SCANDINAVIAN
Cooking

Beatrice Ojakangas

Published by HPBooks
P.O. Box 5367, Tucson, AZ 85703 602/888-2150
ISBN O-89586-230-1 Library of Congress Catalog Card Number: 83-80804
© 1983 Fisher Publishing Inc. Printed in U.S.A.

Cover: West-Coast Salad, page 115.

Beatrice Ojakangas has a rich background in Scandinavian cuisines, traditions and history. She and her husband, Richard, are second-generation Americans. All of their grandparents came from Finland. As they visited in Finland, Beatrice, known as "Peaches" to her friends and relatives, became interested in the foods and traditions of all Scandinavian countries. She has a special knack for making friends, and now has many acquaintances throughout Scandinavia. She is known for the sumptuous smörgåsbords she prepares and serves in her home. If you visit in northern Minnesota, you may find her teaching cooking classes in her large, well-stocked kitchen. Or she may be assisting with Scandinavian heritage-appreciation camps. Beatrice has authored a Finnish cookbook and numerous articles on Finnish and Scandinavian cooking.

◆

The author is grateful to the following: Ruth Kielland, Norwegian Dairies Association; Maria Bøgvald and Jytte Nipper, Danish Dairies; Marja Pekkala of Valio, Finnish Dairies; Marjatta Pauloff, of Arabia of Finland; Kaija Aarikka, of Finland; Gudrun Hoivik, Ivan Nylander and Lise Gindy, readers for languages; Sally Arntson, Helen Gildseth, Esther Luoma and friends and relatives who shared ideas and taste-tested recipes and menus for this book.

Special thanks go to Maid of Scandinavia, Minneapolis; Kaj Dahl of Scandinavian Center, Los Angeles; Arabia of Finland, Niles, Illinios; and to Norwegian & Swedish Imports, Duluth.

CONTENTS

ANOTHER BESTSELLING VOLUME FROM HPBOOKS

Publishers: Bill and Helen Fisher; Executive Editor: Rick Bailey;
Editorial Director: Helen Fisher; Editor: Carroll Latham;
Art Director: Don Burton; Book Design: Kathleen Koopman;
Food Stylist: Carol Peterson;
Photography: George deGennaro Studios

SCANDINAVIAN COOKING

Each Scandinavian country has a personality and cuisine of its own. The differences among the four countries represent ways of life fashioned by people adapting themselves to their own climate, natural resources and terrain.

The backbone of Norwegian cuisine is wonderfully fresh fish and seafood. But it also includes the Norwegians' skill with dairy products. Denmark, the country most influenced by continental cuisine, offers a flower-garden of *smørrebrød* and other beautifully presented food.

Sweden, the bountiful, is lavish with pork, dairy products and wonderful baked goods. Sweden gave the world the *Smörgåsbord*, or *Bread & Butter Table*. The basic idea has spread throughout Scandinavia, so that all kinds of *tables* are set. As you travel, you might begin the day with a *Breakfast Table*. When you visit a home, a *Coffeetable* may be waiting for you. If you're invited to lunch, a *Sandwich Table* might be served. Or, the food at a cocktail party may be served as a *Cheese Table*.

Finland has blended influences from Sweden and Russia into its cuisine, but maintains an earthiness native to itself. Karelian pastries of rye and rice, three-meat ragout, rye and barley breads and fish-filled pies, reflect the abundance of whole grains and fish, and a knack for baking. Thick soups, hearty breads, fruit puddings, buttery pastries and cookies, cardamom-flavored coffee breads and spice cakes are healthy and down-to-earth.

The roots of Scandinavian cuisine lie in the climate and its northern position. People have always had to stock supplies for long winters. Processes of preserving meat, fish, vegetables and fruit have been developed into a fine art. Salting, dehydrating and curing of foods were developed by the Vikings a thousand years ago, in preparation for their long voyages.

Although we think of the Vikings as Norwegians, they came from over the entire Scandinavian peninsula. During the Viking Era, 800 A.D. to 1050 A.D., there were no borders separating Norway, Sweden, Denmark and Finland. With practically inexhaustible manpower, Viking plunderers set out on raids, near and far. The word *vikingar* translates to *pirate*. The British Isles and France suffered Viking incursions. Some reports indicate they made their way as far south as the Mediterranean.

Viking power in Scandinavia was followed by Swedish power and wars between Denmark, Norway and Sweden. Independence came to Denmark in 1665 and to Norway in 1903. Finland was a part of Sweden for 600 years, and was conquered by Russia in 1809. In 1917, Finland obtained its freedom.

Norwegian, Swedish and Danish languages share linguistic ties. They are Germanic languages. The Finnish language bears no resemblance to Norwegian, Swedish or Danish. Finns have always felt their language held them apart—so much so that Bishop Agricola, who brought Christianity to Finland, had to convince them that God could understand Finnish.

Although Iceland shares cultural and lingual ties with Norway and Denmark, its cuisine is not included in this book. Geographically, Finland isn't Scandinavian. But its past, present and future have close ties, culturally and historically with Scandinavia. This book deals with the cuisines and customs of those countries that share borders—Norway, Sweden and Finland—and Denmark, which geographically, is almost an extension of Sweden. This region is often, and more accurately, called *Fennoscandia*.

Because the gulf stream sweeps past the Scandinavian countries, and their summer days are long, the climate is temperate enough to raise a variety of food crops. The crops vary somewhat according to the terrain. Denmark, with no mountains, produces field crops and dairy products. The Danes export a wide variety of cheese and pork products. Sweden also depends on dairying and field crops, but has some fishing industry. Norway is mountainous with deep fjords and inlets. It relies heavily on its fishing industry, but also has a very efficient agricultural program. A great deal of cheese is produced for export. Finland exports a large amount of cheese and other food products. These countries produce about the same kinds of food products, but in varying amounts.

The ancient tradition of handicrafts is closely related to the aesthetic art of food preparation. This includes woodcarving, metalwork, weaving, embroidery and rosemaling. Ordinary, everyday articles are decorated because they are considered more enjoyable to use. The handle of a wooden spoon might be carved with fanciful designs. An engraved brooch might be used to hold an apron strap. Cupboard doors and chairs in Norway may be *rosemaled*—painted or carved with colorful floral or other designs.

Much of Scandinavian cookery has been a well-kept secret. A story is told about a tourist in Oslo who asked a boy, "Where is a good place to eat?" The boy answered, "Best place I've found is right at home." Although there are some fine restaurants in Scandinavia, they do not serve the kind of food that is eaten every day in homes.

Restaurants serve more European fare than Scandinavian specialties. They reflect French and German influence. In Helsinki, Finland, there are several fine Russian restaurants, though Russian food is seldom seen in the average home. Pizza parlors, hamburger stands, ice-cream parlors and European-style coffee houses are scattered throughout cities in all countries.

Scandinavian chefs feel free to adapt the foreign classics to their own available ingredients. As a tourist, this makes eating out rather interesting. You might have a dish such as Potatoes Anna, or a Veal Oscar flavored with allspice and onions—a deviation from authentic dishes. You may find the same dishes in any of the countries. The names and spellings may differ slightly from one village to the next or from one country to another.

Delicate homemade Scandinavian pastries, grain-rich breads, buttery cookies, feathery cakes, homemade cheese, slowly simmered ragouts, light-textured meat and fish loaves, fresh berry desserts, vegetable platters and seasonal salads are better than those we found in restaurants. In fact, the bakery section of a Scandinavian church bazaar is the best showcase for specialties. The local bakery cannot compete with homemade crisp buttery *sandbakkelsers, pepperkaker, goro, rosettes, æbleskiver,* cardamom breads and other delicacies.

Meals in Scandinavian homes feature the best of what is in season. Scandinavians prefer to serve seasonal foods in season. New potatoes might make a whole meal when they are available. A drizzle of butter, perhaps with a sprinkling of fresh dill, is the only adornment. Fresh strawberries in season are served with cream and sugar, or mixed with whipped cream and generously stuffed between layers of sponge cake.

Scandinavians are master bakers, and everyday cooking is far from bland because they use common ingredients in creative ways. There is always good bread and something sweet or savory to go with coffee. Food is usually baked, braised, simmered or pan-fried, but seldom deep-fried. Historically, it was only after the holiday slaughtering they had rendered lard available for deep-frying. Today, lard and vegetable shortening are used mainly to deep-fry certain holiday specialties such as rosettes.

Fresh dill is the favorite herb of Scandinavia, but whole peppercorns, whole allspice, dill seeds, fennel, caraway, cardamom, saffron, nutmeg and cinnamon are used, alone or in combination, to produce new flavors. Dill and ground white pepper might flavor sliced cucumbers or fish, onion and allspice season simmered meats, and a combination of orange peel, caraway, fennel and anise seeds are the classic seasonings for Swedish Limpa and a Finnish Christmas rye bread. Coffee breads are flavored with the sweet spices— cardamom, saffron, nutmeg or cinnamon. Almonds are the favorite nut, especially when used as almond paste, in fillings for breads, cookies, cakes and other pastries. Both salt and sugar are used conservatively in Scandinavia.

Arctic cloudberries have a self-preserving quality and can be enjoyed the year around without much more preparation than to pack them into jars. Lingonberries preserve well, too, and are used much as cranberries are used. For generations, rose hips, known for their high vitamin C content, have been preserved by nutrition-conscious homemakers. Cheesemaking has always been important in Scandinavia. Every dairy farm formerly made its own cheese. Today, cheesemaking is left to immaculate creameries strategically located throughout all countries. A large percentage of Scandinavian cheese is exported.

A good Scandinavian cook has a flair for color, texture, shape and stark simplicity in presenting food. Danes tend to lead in the *fearless combinations* department. For example, a *smørrebrød,* or open-face sandwich, may be topped with cheese, green pepper and sliced fresh strawberries! Finns lead in the *earthy, chewy, whole-grain bread* department. The simplicity of Finnish Rye-Meal Bread magnifies the flavor of the whole-rye grain.

Each of the recipes in this book is labeled with a foreign title and a country of origin. You may find a dish that is equally important in a different country. Even as a researcher in Scandinavia, it has been impossible to find where some dishes originated.

Most of these recipes came from friends in Scandinavian countries, gathered during several trips. Other recipes have come from friends, relatives and my personal collection.

As much as possible, I have used ingredients commonly available in supermarkets. Some ingredients are difficult to find substitutes for, so descriptions and mail-order sources are listed for these items. Special Scandinavian equipment is necessary for some pastries and breads. All are available by mail order or in Scandinavian specialty-cookware shops.

Most of the menus have several choices for each course. Use the menus to give you ideas for entertaining, as well as ideas for adding spark to your family meals.

SCANDINAVIAN EQUIPMENT & INGREDIENTS

The following list of tools, equipment and special ingredients will help to make Scandinavian dishes authentic. A list of mail-order sources for specialty items is on page 154. The items each source handles may vary from time to time. Write to each of them for a list of items, prices and ordering instructions.

Equipment

AEbleskiver or Munk's Pan: Heavy cast-iron or cast-aluminum with round cups. Used to make ball-shape Danish pancakes, sometimes called *munks* or *doughnuts*. The pan will season itself with use, but vegetable shortening, butter or lard is generally used in the cups at each baking. As the batter cooks, it rises. As one side bakes, a filling of chopped apple, applesauce or jam may be spooned into the center. Add enough additional batter to enclose the filling. Use a metal knitting needle or a wooden skewer to turn the pancake ball over. Immediately after each use, wash the pan in warm sudsy water; rinse and dry. See Danish Pancake Balls, page 122.

Goro Iron: Cast-iron or cast-aluminum, this hinged, patterned Norwegian cookie iron is used to make thin, flat rectangles that break into three cookies. Brush the inside of the iron with butter or vegetable shortening when baking the first few cookies. Immediately after each use, wash the iron in warm, sudsy water; rinse and dry. To store the iron, place folded paper towels between the top and bottom plates. See Cardamom Crackers, page 64.

Hardtack or Knäckebröd Rolling Pin: This wooden rolling pin has a hob-nail roller used to make a pattern in the dough when rolling out flatbreads. See Rye & Wheat Flatbread, page 31.

Heart-Shape Waffle Iron: Cast-iron or cast-aluminum waffle plates are shaped like five small hearts. Some irons have non-stick finishes. Some are electric, but traditionally, they are heated on the stove-top. Some are equipped with a cradle support for easy turning. Brush both plates with butter or vegetable shortening each time you add batter. Immediately after each use, wash the iron in warm, sudsy water; rinse and dry. To store the iron, place folded paper towels between the top and bottom plates. See Heart-Shape Waffles, page 13, or use any waffle batter.

Karelian Rolling Pin: Long, slender, Finnish rolling pin, usually made of light birch. The pin is thicker in the center, making it easier to spin the dough as it is rolled out. See Karelian Pies, page 90.

Kransekake or Ring Pans: Set of 18 individual rings or 6 pans with 3 rings. Ring sizes vary from 2-3/8 inches to 7-3/4 inches in diameter. Grease each ring before using. Used to make the towering Norwegian or Scandinavian celebration cake. Immediately after each use, wash the rings in warm, sudsy water; rinse and dry.

Krumkaker or Krumkake Iron: Hinged, patterned, cast-iron or cast-aluminum Norwegian iron used to make thin, round, five- to six-inch cookies. Use vegetable shortening, butter or lard each time the pan is used. It will season itself. Too much butter or shortening will run out onto the stove. Immediately after each use, wash the iron in warm, sudsy water; rinse and dry. To store the iron, place folded paper towels between the top and bottom plates. See Krumbcakes, page 150.

Lefse Rolling Pin: Norwegian rolling pin with long grooves along either the length of the roller or around the roller. Used for rolling out Norwegian *lefse,* a thin flatbread baked on a griddle. See Potato Flatbread and Rye & Wheat Flatbread, page 31, and Mrs. Olson's Flour Lefse, page 124.

Plättar or Plette Pan: Cast-iron or cast-aluminum Swedish pan with shallow, round indentations for making thin pancakes about three inches in diameter. Use vegetable shortening, butter or lard each time the pan is used. It will season itself. Immediately after each use, wash the pan in warm sudsy water; rinse and dry. See Swedish Pancakes, page 14.

Rosette Irons: Used to make fragile deep-fried patty shells or cookie-like pastries. Usually comes in a set of three or four irons with a removable handle. Additional irons are available. Some handles have two arms and will cook two designs at one time. Immediately after each use, wash the irons in warm, sudsy water; rinse and dry. See Rosettes, page 153.

Sandbakelser, Sandbakkel or Tart Tins: Fluted, slant-side Swedish tartlet tins commonly used in all Scandinavian countries to make tart shells or cookies. The tins come in several sizes. Sets usually include from 12 to 18 tins. Immediately after each use, wash the tins in warm, sudsy water; rinse and dry. Stack one inside another to store. See Savory Tartlets, page 71, and Butter-Cookie Shells, page 151.

Special Foods & Ingredients

If some of the following foods are not available in your local supermarket, check local specialty food stores. Also see the mail-order list, page 154, for Scandinavian tools, special equipment and imported Scandinavian ingredients.

Cardamom: Aromatic spice commonly used in pastries and yeast breads. Cardamom pods and ground cardamom are available in most well-stocked supermarkets. Because it loses its pungency quickly after being ground, commercially ground cardamom has a mild flavor. It is best to purchase whole, white, papery, cardamom pods. Use a mortar and pestle to crush the pods. Blow gently on the pod and seeds to remove the pieces of pod. Then crush the small black, aromatic seeds. Or, place the seeds between sheets of plastic or waxed paper and crush with blows of a mallet or hammer.

Cloudberries: These yellow Arctic berries resemble raspberries with lots of seeds. Preserved berries are available in 16-ounce jars. Used for cake fillings, sauces for desserts and fillings for tarts.

Lingonberries: Small, round red berries, tart and much like cranberries in flavor. In some supermarkets, they can be purchased in bulk, sweetened or unsweetened, or preserved in 16-ounce jars. Lingonberries are served with meats, game and poultry dishes.

Pearl Sugar: A confectionery sugar used for decorating coffee breads and cookies. The texture is coarse and can be simulated by coarsely crushing sugar cubes. Imported from Sweden.

Pickled Herring: There is a wide variety of herring packed in wine sauce, dill sauce or brine. It may be cut in tidbits, chunks or fillets. These are usually served directly from the container, but may be seasoned and spiced.

Swedish Anchovies or Baltic Sprats: Do not confuse with smaller, saltier, Portuguese-style anchovies. Available in Scandinavian fish markets or Scandinavian specialty stores. They must be refrigerated. Fillets are available in flat, 3- to 3-1/2-ounce tins. Also available whole, packed in brine and in 6- to 8-ounce jars.

Salted or Brined Whole Herring: Any herring that is packed in salt brine can be used in recipes calling for salted herring. Before using, soak them in cold water for several hours to remove excess salt. Available in delicatessens and fish stores as well as in Scandinavian specialty foods markets.

Swedish Brown Beans (Bruna Bönor): Small, oval, Swedish-grown brown beans. Pinto beans or Great Northern beans may be substituted, but are not the same in flavor or texture. Dried beans are available in Scandinavian specialty stores.

Veal Terrine (Sylta): Shredded meat set in jellied beef broth. Served as a cold-cut during holidays. Can be purchased sliced or in bulk in Scandinavian specialty stores.

BREAKFASTS & BRUNCHES
❧ Farmhouse Brunch ❧

Several years ago in the home of relatives in Western Finland, I admired a mammoth brick range with its bread-baking oven. We sat at the painted wooden kitchen table, enjoying fresh-baked *Pulla,* a cardamom-flavored coffee bread. Behind us ticked an hour-glass-shaped grandfather clock. Since then, because of a desire for the new and modern, many people have removed the old brick ranges and ovens and replaced them with modern electric ranges. I was happy to learn recently that some of the lovely old farmhouses are being renovated and the big brick ranges, complete with bread ovens, are being restored.

Illalla perunavoi, aamulla klapsakkaa, ei emäntä kulta siillä jaksakkaa. "In the evening, mashed potatoes, in the morning potato broth. No my dear wife, I cannot work on just that." This old quote from a Finnish farmer to his wife tells us several things about the past. The hard-working farmer needed substantial food—meat and potatoes—for his breakfast. And the thrifty Finnish wife was using creativity with the simplest of ingredients—leftover potatoes and milk.

Many Scandinavian farmers now supplement their income with jobs away from their fields and forests. Their wives may also be working. Meal patterns have changed from the traditional early morning coffee, breakfast at 11:00 a.m., coffee at 4:00 p.m. and dinner at 5:00 p.m.. Today, because of working away from the farm, they have three meals—breakfast, lunch and dinner.

In the summer, whether at home or visiting friends or relatives, breakfast is simple. You may have a bowl of fresh berries from the garden or from a colorful open-market stall. The fruit is served with bread, butter and coffee. In the winter, the fruit may be a bowl of preserved cloudberries, stewed prunes, applesauce or fresh lingonberries—available all year in Scandinavia.

The following menu combines elements from several Scandinavian countries. Today, it is not uncommon for a traveler to find Norwegian foods in Finland and Danish or Swedish foods in Norway. There is a free exchange of recipes and ideas throughout Scandinavia, mostly due to the great number of food-related magazines available.

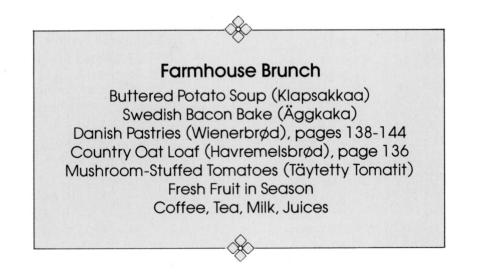

Farmhouse Brunch
Buttered Potato Soup (Klapsakkaa)
Swedish Bacon Bake (Äggkaka)
Danish Pastries (Wienerbrød), pages 138-144
Country Oat Loaf (Havremelsbrød), page 136
Mushroom-Stuffed Tomatoes (Täytetty Tomatit)
Fresh Fruit in Season
Coffee, Tea, Milk, Juices

Mushroom-Stuffed Tomatoes

Täytetty Tomatit — Finland

Colorful and a satisfying brunch dish.

8 medium tomatoes
2 cups finely chopped mushrooms
1 cup whipping cream
1 cup finely chopped sweet onion
3 tablespoons fresh lemon juice

2 tablespoons Dijon-style mustard
1/2 teaspoon ground white pepper
1/2 to 1 teaspoon salt
Parsley sprigs or leaf lettuce for garnish,
   if desired

Cut a 1/4-inch slice off bottom of each tomato. Reserve slices; keep with tomatoes from which they were cut. Scoop seeds and pulp from center of tomatoes. Arrange tomatoes and reserved slices, cut-side down, on paper towels, to drain. Wrap mushrooms in paper towels to remove as much moisture as possible. In a medium bowl, whip cream until soft peaks form. Fold in dry mushrooms, onion, lemon juice, mustard, white pepper and salt to taste. Spoon into tomatoes. On top of each, insert reserved slices vertically into mushroom mixture. Garnish with parsley or lettuce, if desired. Arrange stuffed tomatoes on a platter. Makes 8 servings.

Swedish Bacon Bake

Äggkaka — Sweden

Prepare this baked omelet the night before and bake it at the last minute.

1 lb. sliced bacon
1/2 lb. mushrooms, sliced
3 tablespoons butter, if desired
2 tablespoons cornstarch
2 cups half and half

18 eggs
1 teaspoon salt
1/2 teaspoon dried leaf tarragon
1-1/2 cups shredded Emmentaler or
   Jarlsberg cheese (6 oz.)

Butter a shallow 2- to 3-quart casserole dish; set aside. Cut bacon slices in half. In a large skillet, cook bacon over medium heat until crisp. Drain on paper towels. Increase heat to high. Pour off all but about 3 tablespoons bacon drippings. Sauté mushrooms in bacon drippings until mushrooms are lightly browned, about 3 minutes. Or, if desired, melt butter in a large skillet; sauté mushrooms in melted butter. Stir in cornstarch until evenly distributed. Slowly stir in half and half until blended. Cook and stir until thickened. In a large bowl, beat eggs until blended. Stir in 1 or 2 cups mushroom mixture. Stir egg mixture into remaining mushroom mixture. Scramble over medium heat only until eggs begin to set; do not cook completely. Stir in salt and tarragon. Pour partially cooked egg mixture into prepared casserole dish. Sprinkle cheese over top. Overlap cooked bacon slices around edge. Cover and refrigerate overnight, if desired, or bake immediately. **To bake immediately,** preheat oven to 300F (150C). Bake 30 minutes or until casserole is heated through and cheese is melted. **To bake after being refrigerated,** preheat oven to 300F (150C); bake 45 minutes. Makes 8 to 10 generous servings.

How to Make Mushroom-Stuffed Tomatoes

1/Cut a 1/4-inch slice from bottom of each tomato. Scoop out pulp and seeds from center.

2/Spoon filling into hollow tomatoes. Insert reserved slices in filling so they stand up.

Buttered Potato Soup

Klapsakkaa—Finland

Make this creamy soup with last night's potatoes and serve it steaming hot in mugs.

2 cups mashed potatoes
4 cups milk
2 cups half and half
Salt and pepper to taste

Dash ground allspice
About 2 tablespoons chopped fresh parsley
About 4 teaspoons butter

In a medium saucepan, beat potatoes and milk with a whisk until smooth. Stir in half and half. Stir over medium heat until soup barely comes to a boil. Add salt and pepper to taste. Sprinkle top with a dash of allspice. Ladle into individual bowls or mugs. Garnish each with parsley and 1/2 teaspoon butter. Serve immediately. Makes 8 servings.

❖ Summertime Garden Breakfast ❖

Scandinavian long summer days have a few hours of silver twilight that mark the nighttime. By two in the morning, birds are awake and calling each other, their resonant voices somehow amplified in the wooded surroundings. In gardens, roses bloom among the irises, peonies and lupins. A Scandinavian summer garden is an inspiring place to have a leisurely breakfast.

In the summer, one might be invited to a midnight coffee party that continues until breakfast. The party is usually held at the host's summertime retreat—a cabin or mountain hut—away from the bustle of city life. Businesses often close for an entire month to let their employees fully enjoy summer. It is an inconvenient time to try to do business, but a wonderful time to have friends with a summer house.

Berries and garden vegetables ripen quickly in the intensity of long summer days. Dairy herds are at their peak production and supplies of dairy products are plentiful.

When the day will be spent at home, most Scandinavians begin their day with early morning coffee and a piece of cardamom-perfumed bread, a crisp rusk or a slice of rye bread topped with a shaving of cheese. On a Scandinavian farm, breakfast is served at about 11:00 a.m. This full, hot meal usually includes boiled potatoes, a meat dish, bread, cheese and perhaps a fruit pudding for dessert.

Heart-Shape Waffles are a many-season favorite in Norway, but are a special spring and summer treat. In Sweden, these waffles are traditionally served on Lady Day, March 25—formally known as Annunciation Day. This is exactly nine months before Christmas. These special waffles are delicious served hot, but are usually served cold. Be sure to cover them with plastic wrap and refrigerate them so they won't dry out before you serve them. No matter how much cream is in the batter, Scandinavians still prefer their waffles served with whipped cream and berries!

Summertime Garden Breakfast

Raspberry Nectar (Hallonsaft)
Samsø Soufflé (Samsøsouffle)
Heart-Shape Waffles (Fløtevafler)
or
Swedish Pancakes (Plättar)
Whipped Cream, Fresh Berries or Other Fruit
Milk, Fruit Juice, Coffee, Tea

Raspberry Nectar

Hallonsaft—Sweden

After adding water, serve this clear red nectar over ice in stemmed glasses.

4 qts. red raspberries	**2 cups water**
2 cups white-wine vinegar	**About 4 cups sugar**

In a large glass jar or bowl, combine raspberries, vinegar and water. Let stand overnight. Wash 4 pint jars in hot soapy water; rinse. Keep hot. Prepare self-sealing lids as manufacturer directs. Pour raspberry mixture into a large saucepan. Stirring occasionally, bring to a boil over medium heat; boil 1 minute. Line a strainer with several layers of damp cheesecloth or a damp muslin towel; place over a large bowl. Pour mixture into lined strainer. Let juice drip through lined strainer; do not squeeze. Measure juice; return juice to pan. For each cup of juice, add 3/4 cup sugar. Stirring constantly, bring to a boil over medium heat; boil 10 minutes. Pour juice into 1 hot jar at a time, leaving 1/4 inch headspace. Wipe rim of jar with a clean damp cloth. Attach lid. Place in a water-bath canner or a pot large enough to hold jars covered with boiling water. Fill and close remaining jars. After water comes to a boil, begin timing. Process 15 minutes, adding 1 minute for each 1000 feet of altitude above sea level. Cool on a rack, away from drafts, 10 to 12 hours. Do not tighten rings of self-sealing lids. Check lids for seal. If jars did not seal, store in refrigerator. To serve, add 1/4 cup nectar to 1 pint water. Adjust amount of nectar to taste. Pour over ice cubes in drinking glasses. Makes 4 pints.

Heart-Shape Waffles   Photo on page 15.

Fløtevafler—Norway

Delicious hot, but usually served cold.

5 eggs	**1 cup dairy sour cream, stirred**
1/2 cup sugar	**1/4 cup unsalted butter, melted**
1/2 teaspoon salt	**Fresh lingonberries or other berries or fruit**
1 teaspoon ground cardamom	**Whipped cream**
1 cup all-purpose flour	

In large bowl of electric mixer, beat eggs and sugar on high speed until mixture forms ribbons when beaters are lifted from bowl, about 10 minutes. Beat in salt and cardamom. Sprinkle flour over surface of batter. Use a rubber spatula to fold in flour, then fold in sour cream and butter. Let mixture stand 10 minutes. Preheat heart-shape waffle iron according to manufacturer's directions. Pour about 3/4 cup batter onto center of waffle iron. Close top; bake 2 to 3 minutes on each side over medium heat until waffle is golden and crisp. Serve immediately with berries or other fruit and whipped cream. Or, cool waffles on a rack and serve cold. Makes about 8 waffles or 40 heart-shape pieces.

Samsø Soufflé

Samsøsouffle—Denmark

You can prepare this soufflé, freeze it, then bake it later—but it will have a coarse texture.

1 cup half and half	1/2 teaspoon salt
1/4 cup all-purpose flour	1/4 teaspoon white pepper
2 tablespoons butter	4 eggs, separated
1 cup shredded samsø or tybo cheese (4 oz.)	1/8 teaspoon cream of tartar

Butter a 1- to 1-1/2-quart soufflé dish; set aside. In a medium saucepan, combine half and half and flour. Beat with a whisk until smooth. Over medium heat, stir with a whisk until mixture comes to a boil. Add butter. Cook and stir until mixture thickens. Stir in cheese, salt and white pepper. In a small bowl, beat egg yolks until blended. Stir in about 1/2 cup cheese sauce. Stir egg-yolk mixture into remaining cheese sauce; set aside. In a medium bowl, beat egg whites until frothy. Add cream of tartar; continue beating until whites form short, soft but distinctive peaks. Tips of peaks will bend over. Fold into cheese sauce. Pour cheese mixture into prepared dish. Bake or cover and freeze. **To bake immediately,** preheat oven to 375F (190C). Bake 30 to 35 minutes or until puffed and golden. Soufflé will be soft in center. **To bake after freezing,** preheat oven to 350F (175C). Remove cover from soufflé dish; place frozen soufflé in preheated oven. Bake 45 to 60 minutes. Makes 4 servings.

Swedish Pancakes

Plättar—Sweden

So light that Swedes say they should "fly off the griddle."

1 egg	1 tablespoon sugar
3/4 cup milk	2 tablespoons butter, melted
1/4 teaspoon salt	Lingonberry jam or other jam or jelly
1/2 cup all-purpose flour	Dairy sour cream
1 teaspoon baking powder	

Preheat *plättar pan,* page 7, over medium heat. In a large bowl, beat egg; stir in milk, salt, flour, baking powder and sugar until batter is smooth. Stir in melted butter. Grease cups in hot pan with shortening or butter. Spoon 2 rounded tablespoons batter into each greased cup. Cook about 1 minute on each side or until golden brown. Serve immediately with jam or jelly and sour cream. Makes 20 pancakes.

 If a recipe calls for room-temperature eggs and yours are cold, fill a bowl with hot tap water. Immerse the eggs in the water and let stand 3 to 4 minutes. Separated egg whites and yolks can be warmed by placing them in bowls over warm water.

Samsø Soufflé with Heart-Shape Waffles, page 13.

SMØRREBRØD— OPEN-FACE SANDWICHES

❖ Smørrebrød Sampler ❖

Shrimp and other shellfish are abundant along the seacoasts of Scandinavia. One can walk along the pier of a seacoast village in Norway or Denmark, buy a sack of freshly cooked shrimp, and shell them as you would peanuts. Pop the delicious morsels into your mouth, then drop the shells into the water for scavenger fish to devour. They also make excellent *smørrebrød*.

Although smørrebrød originated in Denmark, they can become a sampling of Scandinavian flavors. Herring, onion, salted salmon, shrimp, beef and many other ingredients are classic smørrebrød fare. Smørrebrød have become popular throughout Scandinavia. Tourists can walk into any coffee bar and find simple or elaborate open-face sandwiches.

When you plan a whole meal of smørrebrød, follow the pattern for a regular menu, planning two, three or four courses. Start with a first course of fish, followed with meat or poultry for the main course. Smørrebrød may be served for all courses, even dessert. However, in Denmark, dessert is usually a fruit or cream pudding with a cookie, Danish pastry or cream cake. Dessert smørrebrød may be cheese, nuts and fruit, singly or in combination. Schnapps or Aquavit, followed by beer as a chaser, is appropriate even at lunch.

This menu offers flexibility. Choose one or more of the smørrebrød from each course. Serve each course separately. Or, offer all of the smørrebrød at the same luncheon. For a cooperative effort, ask each guest to bring one smørrebrød to be sampled. All the smørrebrød can be made ahead and refrigerated overnight.

How to Make Smørrebrød

1/Use compact loaves of homemade or commercial bread that hold their shape when cut. Dark breads, firm pumpernickels or firm slices of French bread are best. Day-old bread is better than freshly baked bread. Slice all dark breads 1/4 to 3/8 inch thick. Remove the crusts. Slice French bread about 1/2 inch thick. Do not remove the crusts.

2/Arrange slices of bread on a flat surface. Butter each slice, covering to all edges. This will prevent moist toppings from soaking through. Add each topping and garnish to all slices of bread before adding the next topping or garnish.

3/Place a leaf of lettuce on one end or corner of the buttered bread, gathering it so it takes up little space. The lettuce should not cover the entire slice of bread.

4/Cover remaining bread with thinly sliced fish, meat or vegetables.

5/Garnish with red and green vegetables or fruits such as radish slices, parsley sprigs, watercress, bean or alfalfa sprouts, tomato pieces or wedges, onion rings, cucumber twists, orange or lemon twists.

Smørrebrød Sampler

First Course:
Onion & Herring Smørrebrød (Sild med Løg)
Cream-Cheese & Salmon Smørrebrød (Flødeost med Laks)
Dilled-Shrimp Smørrebrød (Rejer i Trængsel)

Main Course:
Chicken & Cucumber Smørrebrød (Kylling med Agurke)
Beef & Onion Smørrebrød (Oksesteg med Løg)
Roast-Pork Smørrebrød (Flæskesteg)
Egg & Caviar Smørrebrød (AEg med Kaviar)

Dessert Course:
Red-Berry Pudding (Rødgrød)
or
Danish Rum Cream (Romfromage)
Vanilla Wreaths (Vanillekranser), page 147
Caroline's Apple Cake (Karolines AEblekage)
Danish Beer, Schnapps, Coffee, Tea

Egg & Caviar Smørrebrød

AEg med Kaviar—Denmark

It is traditional to cut the crusts from most breads to give the smørrebrød an even edge.

4 slices Danish Pumpernickel, page 135,
  or other rye bread
4 teaspoons butter
2 tablespoons mayonnaise

4 hard-cooked eggs, sliced
2 tablespoons red or black lumpfish,
  salmon or sturgeon caviar
Parsley

Cut crusts from bread. Spread 1 teaspoon butter on each slice of bread, covering completely. Cut each buttered slice in half crosswise or into 4'' x 2'' pieces. Spread each with mayonnaise, then top with egg slices. Dot each egg slice with caviar. Garnish with parsley. Makes 8 sandwiches.

Onion & Herring Smørrebrød

Sild med Løg—Denmark

Herring and onion smørrebrød is the favorite of all combinations!

4 slices Danish Pumpernickel, page 135,
   or other rye bread
4 teaspoons butter, softened
1 (8-oz.) jar herring fillets in wine sauce

1 medium, sweet onion, cut in thin rings
8 thin tomato wedges
Watercress or parsley

Cut crusts from bread. Spread 1 teaspoon butter on each slice of bread, covering completely. Cut each buttered slice in half crosswise; trim to make 4" x 2" rectangles. Drain fish; cut in 1-inch strips. Top each piece of bread with one-eighth of herring, placing fish smooth-side up. Top each with several onion rings and 1 tomato wedge. Garnish each with watercress or parsley. Makes 8 sandwiches.

Cream-Cheese & Salmon Smørrebrød

Flødeost med Laks—Denmark

Use your own homemade Salted Salmon, page 113, or purchase it at a delicatessen.

4 slices Danish Pumpernickel, page 135, or
   other rye bread
4 teaspoons butter

2 oz. cream cheese, softened
3 oz. thinly sliced smoked or salted salmon
16 paper-thin cucumber slices

Cut crusts from bread. Spread 1/2 teaspoon butter on each piece of bread, covering completely. Cut each buttered slice in half crosswise; trim to make 3" x 2" rectangles. Spread each with cream cheese, covering completely. Top each with salmon, laying salmon flat. Top each with 2 cucumber slices, gathering slices in a mound. Makes 8 sandwiches.

Dilled-Shrimp Smørrebrød

Rejer i Trængsel—Denmark

Purchase frozen tiny shrimp that are already cooked.

2 thin lemon slices
3 tablespoons butter, softened
8 slices French bread
1 cup mayonnaise
1 teaspoon dried dill weed

8 small butter- or leaf-lettuce leaves
1/2 lb. tiny cooked shrimp, thawed if frozen
8 thin tomato wedges
8 tiny parsley sprigs

Cut lemon slices in quarters; set aside. Spread about 1 teaspoon butter on each slice of bread, covering completely. Spread each with 2 tablespoons mayonnaise; sprinkle each with dill weed. Place 1 lettuce leaf on end of each slice of bread. Divide shrimp among sandwiches, mounding on top of mayonnaise and lettuce. Garnish each with a tomato wedge, piece of lemon and a parsley sprig. Makes 8 sandwiches.

Smørrebrød at top: Cheese & Strawberry, Cheese & Grape, both page 28; at right: Beef & Onion, page 21; bottom: Dilled Shrimp, Onion & Herring, Smoked Salmon, page 27.

Chicken & Cucumber Smørrebrød

Kylling med Agurke—Denmark

Poached chicken breast and cucumbers on buttered bread make a tasty open-face sandwich.

1 tablespoon sugar
1 teaspoon salt
1/4 cup distilled white vinegar
1/4 cup water
1 (8-inch) European-style cucumber or
   other cucumber, thinly sliced
Poached Chicken Breasts, see below

4 slices Danish Pumpernickel, page 135,
   or other rye bread
4 teaspoons butter, softened
4 butter- or leaf-lettuce leaves
4 thin tomato slices or wedges
4 bacon slices, cooked crisp

Poached Chicken Breasts:
1 chicken breast, halved, skinned, boned
1/2 cup dry white wine

1/2 cup water
1 teaspoon pickling spices

In a medium bowl, combine sugar, salt, vinegar and water. Stir in cucumber. Refrigerate 30 to 60 minutes. Prepare Poached Chicken Breasts; set aside to cool. Cut crusts from bread. Spread 1 teaspoon butter on each slice of bread, covering completely. Gather lettuce leaves in ruffles. Place each ruffled leaf on 1 end of a slice of bread. Place one-fourth of poached-chicken slices on uncovered portion of bread. Drain cucumbers on paper towels; arrange one-fourth of drained cucumbers on each sandwich. Garnish each with a tomato slice or wedge and bacon. Makes 4 sandwiches.

Poached Chicken Breasts:
Place chicken-breast halves in an 8-inch skillet. Add wine, water and pickling spices. Bring to a boil, then simmer over low heat 20 minutes or until meat is firm but not hard. Drain; let cool. Use a sharp knife to slice diagonally across grain, as thinly as possible.

Roast-Pork Smørrebrød

Flæskesteg—Denmark

Pork, pickled cabbage and prunes—who but the Danes would put them together?

8 slices Danish Pumpernickel, page 135,
   or other rye bread
8 teaspoons butter, softened
8 small butter- or leaf-lettuce leaves
8 thin slices roast pork (about 1/2 lb.)

1/2 cup drained, canned, sweet-sour red
   cabbage, chilled
8 cooked prunes, pitted
8 thin slices peeled orange
8 parsley sprigs

Cut crusts from bread. Spread 1 teaspoon butter on each slice of bread, covering completely. Press a small lettuce leaf onto 1 end of each buttered slice. Fold and ruffle sliced pork to cover bread completely. Top each with 1 tablespoon cabbage and 1 pitted prune. Cut each orange slice from outside edge to center; twist. Place 1 orange twist on top of each sandwich. Garnish each with parsley. Makes 8 sandwiches.

How to Make Chicken & Cucumber Smørrebrød

1/Poach chicken breasts. Slice cooked breasts diagonally across grain into thin slices.

2/Gather lettuce in ruffles. Place a ruffled leaf on 1 end of each buttered bread.

Beef & Onion Smørrebrød   Photo on page 19.

Oksesteg med Løg—Denmark

The Danes use leftover beef in sandwiches, but the Swedes use it on a smörgåsbord.

**8 slices Danish Pumpernickel, page 135,
  or other rye bread
8 teaspoons butter, softened
1/3 cup Dijon-style mustard
8 thin slices rare roast beef
  (about 1/2 lb.)**

**8 teaspoons dairy sour cream
1/2 cup canned crisp-fried onions, crumbled
8 thin tomato wedges
8 parsley or watercress sprigs**

Cut crusts from bread. Spread 1 teaspoon butter on each slice of bread, covering completely. Spread each generously with mustard. Place 1 slice roast beef on top of each, gathering or ruffling so beef covers bread but does not extend over sides. Top each beef slice with 1 teaspoon sour cream. Sprinkle with crumbled onions; top with a tomato wedge. Garnish with parsley or watercress. Makes 8 sandwiches.

Red-Berry Pudding

Rødgrød—Denmark

This interesting berry pudding has a jelly-like consistency.

1 lb. fresh or frozen unsweetened raspberries,
    strawberries, blackberries or
    boysenberries
About 4 cups water
1/3 cup cornstarch

1 cup sugar
Pinch of salt
1/4 cup sliced almonds, toasted
1 cup whipping cream

In a medium saucepan, combine berries and 4 cups water. Bring to a boil. Simmer over low heat 5 minutes. Place a sieve over a medium bowl. Pour berry mixture into sieve; press with the back of a spoon to remove as much pulp as possible. Discard seeds. Measure juice and pulp. If necessary, add water to make 5 cups. In a small bowl, combine cornstarch with 2/3 cup juice from pulp, making a thin paste. Pour remaining juice and pulp into saucepan; bring to a boil over medium heat, stirring occasionally. Stir in sugar, salt and cornstarch paste. Stirring vigorously with a wooden spoon to keep pudding smooth, cook until thickened. Cover pan; set aside to cool 20 to 30 minutes. Pour cooled pudding into a serving bowl. Sprinkle with sliced almonds. Serve immediately or cover bowl with plastic wrap and refrigerate until served. Pour whipping cream into a small pitcher. Serve pudding warm or cold, with cream. Makes 8 servings.

Danish Rum Cream

Romfromage—Denmark

Rum-flavored desserts became popular when Denmark had colonies in the West Indies.

1 (1/4-oz.) envelope unflavored gelatin
1/4 cup cold water
2 cups milk
4 egg yolks
1/4 cup sugar

1/4 teaspoon salt
1 cup whipping cream
2 tablespoons rum or
    1/4 teaspoon rum extract

Stir gelatin into cold water; set aside to soften 5 minutes. In a medium saucepan, heat milk until surface begins to shimmer. In a small bowl, beat egg yolks, sugar and salt until fluffy. Stir 1/4 cup hot milk into sugar mixture. Whisking constantly, pour sugar mixture into remaining hot milk. Cook and stir 2 minutes or until mixture thickens enough to coat a spoon. Place saucepan with milk mixture in a larger saucepan or sink. Pour cold water into outer container. Stir gelatin into milk mixture. Replacing cold water in outer container as necessary, stir occasionally as milk mixture chills and thickens. Whip cream; fold into chilled milk mixture. Stir in rum or rum extract. Pour into a serving bowl. Cover and refrigerate at least 2 hours before serving. Makes 6 servings.

Red-Berry Pudding; Vanilla Wreaths, page 147.

Caroline's Apple Cake

Karolines Æblekage—Denmark

Apple cakes similar to this are popular all over Scandinavia.

4 to 5 medium Golden Delicious apples
3/4 cup butter, room temperature
3/4 cup sugar
3 eggs, room temperature
1/4 teaspoon salt

1 teaspoon vanilla extract
1-1/2 cups all-purpose flour
2 tablespoons butter, melted
2 tablespoons sugar

Butter an 11-inch tart pan with a removable bottom or a 9-inch square cake pan; set aside. Peel and halve apples. Use a melon baller or a teaspoon to remove cores. Preheat oven to 425F (220C). In a large bowl, cream 3/4 cup butter and 3/4 cup sugar. Beat in eggs, salt and vanilla until light and fluffy. Stir in flour to make a stiff batter. Spread batter in prepared pan. Arrange apples on a flat surface, cut-side down. Cut crosswise incisions almost all the way through each apple half, 1/16 to 1/8 inch apart. Do not cut all the way through. Press apple halves, core-side down, into batter. Brush apples with 2 tablespoons melted butter; sprinkle with 2 tablespoons sugar. Bake 30 minutes or until apples are tender and cake is golden brown. Makes 6 to 8 servings.

How to Make Caroline's Apple Cake

1/Use a melon baller or a teaspoon to remove cores from apple halves.

2/Cut crosswise incisions almost through each apple, 1/16 to 1/8 inch apart.

❧ Smørrebrød to Honor Danish Arts ❧

As our tour bus pulled through the elephant-pillar gates of Carlsberg brewery in Copenhagen, our guide explained that the firm was owned by the state. All profits from the brewery go toward furthering the arts in Denmark. In her gutteral voice, she advised us, ''When you lift your glass of Danish beer, you can always make it a toast to the arts in Denmark!''

What you serve as a drink in Scandinavia depends on whether the person is driving an automobile. There are strict rules that forbid anyone who has had even a drop of anything alcoholic from driving. For this reason, all parties have a non-alcoholic beverage for guests. Those who are walking or are passengers, may choose beer or wine. Mineral water, milk, buttermilk or fruit juices are usually the other choices. Coffee is served after dessert and rarely, if ever, served with a meal.

Soup is often the pre-dinner drink in Scandinavia, served in a mug before you sit down. Danes often surprise us with new ideas. Apples form the basis of the creamy, curry-flavored soup in the menu below. It is served as a separate first course.

Smørrebrød, literally translated, means buttered *(smør)* bread *(brød)*. This Danish open-face sandwich is a culinary cross between a sandwich and a salad. It is a small meal by itself when topped with vegetables, meat, fish, poultry or cheese. It is always eaten on a plate, with a knife and fork, not out-of-hand.

Smørrebrød can be served in different ways. In one Danish home, all ingredients for smørrebrød are served separately. Guests make their own open-face sandwiches. In another home, several types of completed smørrebrød are arranged on a tray. Guests make their own selection. Another method is to have three different smørrebrød on each person's plate. If you want a meal to last a long time, serve the smørrebrød one variety at a time.

Prepared in full, this menu offers an impressive array of colorful smørrebrød. You may want to select one to four varieties from each course and increase the recipes from four to twelve servings.

Smørrebrød to Honor Danish Arts

First Course:
Danish Apple Soup (AEblesuppe) or

Main Course:
Sardine & Onion Smørrebrød (Sardin med Løg)
Smoked-Salmon Smørrebrød (Laks)
Turkey-Lingonberry Smørrebrød (Kalkun)
Ham & Egg Smørrebrød (Skinke med AEg)

Dessert Course:
Cheese & Grape Smørrebrød (Danablu med Frugt)
Cheese & Strawberry Smørrebrød (Flødeost med Jordbær)
Havarti & Marmalade Smørrebrød (Havarti med Nødder)
Schnapps, Beer, Coffee, Tea, Fruit Juice

Danish Apple Soup

Æblesuppe—Denmark

In Denmark, apples are sometimes used as vegetables in soups and salads.

1-1/2 lbs. cooking apples (6 to 8)
5 whole cloves
Water
1 tablespoon lemon juice
2 cups white wine, white-grape juice or
    water

2 tablespoons cornstarch
1 to 2 teaspoons curry powder
1/2 cup whipping cream
3 tablespoons sugar
1 teaspoon butter
1/8 teaspoon salt

Wash and peel apples, reserving peel. Immediately combine peelings, cloves and water to cover in a large saucepan. Over medium-low heat, simmer 30 minutes. While peelings simmer, core and slice apples. Sprinkle with lemon juice to prevent darkening. Place a sieve over a medium bowl. Pour peeling mixture into sieve. Discard peelings and cloves; return broth to saucepan. Add apple slices and 2 cups wine, juice or water. Simmer over low heat 30 minutes or until apples are tender. Puree apple mixture in a blender, adding cornstarch and curry powder during processing. Pour pureed mixture into saucepan. Stir in cream, sugar, butter and salt. Bring to a gentle boil over medium heat. Cook and stir until thickened. Serve hot. Makes 6 servings.

Sardine & Onion Smørrebrød

Sardin med Løg—Denmark

Convenient canned sardines from Denmark or Norway make this smørrebrød quick to prepare.

4 slices Danish Pumpernickel, page 135,
    or other rye bread
4 teaspoons butter, softened
1 (3- to 4-oz.) can sardines, drained

8 stuffed green olives, sliced
4 thin sweet-onion slices
4 fresh dill or parsley sprigs
4 paper-thin lemon slices

Cut crusts from bread. Spread 1 teaspoon butter on each slice of bread, covering completely. Arrange one-fourth of sardines and one-fourth of olives on each piece of bread. Top each with an onion slice. Garnish each with dill or parsley and lemon. Makes 4 sandwiches.

Turkey-Lingonberry Smørrebrød

Kalkun—Denmark

Purchase cooked, thinly sliced turkey from a delicatessen.

4 teaspoons butter, softened
4 slices French bread
2 teaspoons Dijon-style mustard
4 small butter- or leaf-lettuce leaves

4 paper-thin slices cold cooked
    turkey breast
1/4 cup fresh whole lingonberries or
    cooked whole cranberries

Spread 1 teaspoon butter on each slice of bread, covering completely. Spread each with 1/2 teaspoon mustard. Gather lettuce leaves into ruffles; place 1 ruffled leaf on 1 end of each buttered bread. Top each with a slice of turkey breast, letting some of lettuce extend beyond turkey. Garnish with lingonberries or cranberries. Makes 4 sandwiches.

How to Make Smoked-Salmon Smørrebrød

1/Use a sharp knife to cut cucumbers paper-thin. Or slice paper-thin in a food processor.

2/Gather several cucumber slices together and mound on top of fish.

Smoked-Salmon Smørrebrød   Photo on page 19.

Laks—Denmark

Use the thin slicing blade of your food processor to cut paper-thin slices of cucumber.

4 slices Danish Pumpernickel, page 135, or
    French bread
4 teaspoons butter, softened
1 (3-oz.) pkg. cream cheese, softened
4 butter- or leaf-lettuce leaves

1/4 lb. smoked salmon, trout, herring or
    whitefish
1 (5-inch) European-style cucumber or other
    cucumber, sliced paper-thin
4 paper-thin lemon slices, if desired

Cut crusts from pumpernickel, but not from French bread. Spread 1 teaspoon butter on each slice of bread, covering completely. Spread each with cream cheese. Gather lettuce leaves in ruffles. Place each ruffled leaf on 1 end of a slice of bread. Press into cream cheese to hold in place. Flake fish; arrange one-fourth on each sandwich, in an even layer. Gather several cucumber slices in your fingers, ruffling them together. Pile on top of fish. Garnish with a lemon slice. Makes 4 sandwiches.

Ham & Egg Smørrebrød

Skinke med Æg—Denmark

Ham and vegetables make this smørrebrød as colorful as a garden of flowers.

6 slices whole-wheat bread
7 teaspoons butter, softened
1 egg, thoroughly beaten
6 thin, cooked ham slices

12 paper-thin cucumber slices
6 tomato slices
6 butter- or leaf-lettuce leaves
Parsley or watercress

Cut crusts from bread. Spread 1 teaspoon butter on each slice of bread, covering completely; set aside. Over low heat, melt remaining teaspoon butter in a skillet or omelet pan that measures 8 inches across bottom. Add beaten egg; swirl pan until egg covers bottom of pan. Cook only until egg is set and surface feels dry. Cut into 1/2-inch strips; let cool. Roll ham slices into cones. Gather lettuce leaves in ruffles. Place each ruffled leaf on 1 end of a slice of each buttered bread. Place 1 ham cone on part of each slice not covered with lettuce. Loosely roll up cooled egg strips. Place 1 rolled egg strip inside wide end of each ham cone. Cut each cucumber and tomato slice from center to outer edge, cutting through peel. Twist cucumber slices and tomato slices and place on top of ham. Garnish with parsley or watercress. Makes 6 sandwiches.

Cheese & Grape Smørrebrød   Photo on page 19.

Danablu med Frugt—Denmark

This can serve as an excellent dessert smørrebrød for those who don't want sweets.

4 thin slices firm white or French bread
4 teaspoons butter, softened
4 slices Danish blue, mycella or
  other blue cheese (4 oz.)

4 small bunches seedless green grapes

Cut crusts from white bread, but not from French bread. Spread 1 teaspoon butter on each slice of bread, covering completely. Top each with a slice of blue cheese. If bread shows beneath cheese, cut off excess bread or spread cheese to cover. Press 1 bunch of grapes into blue cheese on each sandwich. Makes 4 dessert sandwiches.

Cheese & Strawberry Smørrebrød   Photo on page 19.

Flødeost med Jordbær—Denmark

A marvelous combination of flavors!

4 thin slices firm white or French bread
4 teaspoons butter, softened
1 (3-oz.) pkg. cream cheese, cut in 4 slices

4 crisp green-pepper rings
8 large strawberries, hulled, halved

Cut crusts from white bread, but not from French bread. Spread 1 teaspoon butter on each slice of bread, covering completely. Top each with a slice of cream cheese. Spread cheese, covering bread. Top each with a green-pepper ring and 4 strawberries halves. Makes 4 dessert sandwiches.

How to Make Ham & Egg Smørrebrød

1/Swirl egg in pan until bottom is covered. Cook until egg is set and surface feels dry. Cut in 1/2-inch strips.

2/Roll up egg strips and place in open end of ham cones. Place on buttered bread. Garnish as directed.

Havarti & Walnut Smørrebrød

Havarti med Nødder — Denmark

Use any aged cheese for this dessert smørrebrød.

4 slices firm white or French bread
4 teaspooons butter, softened
4 to 8 slices aged Havarti or other
**   strong-flavor cheese (4 to 6 oz.)**

16 walnut halves
About 3 tablespoons orange marmalade

Cut crusts from white bread, but not from French bread. Spread 1 teaspoon butter on each slice of bread, covering completely. Top each with enough cheese to cover bread completely. Top each with 4 walnut halves. Spoon a small dollop of orange marmalade on top of walnuts. Makes 4 dessert sandwiches.

LUNCHES & SUPPERS
❖ Winter-Fun Party ❖

Scandinavians are avid outdoor-sports fans—never mind the cold winter weather. By February, the days have become longer, though not much warmer. With more daylight hours, people spend time outside, enjoying ice skating and cross-country skiing.

Physical fitness and competition are historically important to Scandinavians, dating back to the Vikings with their superb physical stamina. Annual marathons and races, such as the *Finlandia* ski race, Sweden's *Vaasaloppet* cross-country ski race and the Norwegian *Birkebeiner* race, have inspired similar competitions worldwide.

But outdoor activities are not limited to the professional sportsmen and women. In Denmark, laborers, business people, housewives and school children skate wherever there is ice. Some have lakes and ponds available to them. In the towns, tennis courts and football and soccer fields are flooded to make ice for skating.

Cross-country skiing takes the prize for popularity as a winter sport. As often as they can, Norwegians head for their huts in the mountains for weekends of ski-touring. In Sweden and Finland, they go by airplane or train to the snow-covered slopes of Lapland to enjoy ski holidays and weekends.

If you travel to Finland or Sweden, there are several Lapland resorts where you can stay and enjoy days of cross-country skiing on the sloping *fells* or mountains. In Finland, you can stay in rustic holiday-village log cabins with fully equipped kitchens. Or, you may prefer a country farmhouse on a full-board basis. Accommodations may be simple, but they are immaculate. Meals are enjoyed with the family. Wherever you stay, you'll experience exhilarating sauna baths.

This menu is meant to warm you after a day on the slopes. It can be easily prepared in the simple kitchen of a vacation home or in your own home.

Winter-Fun Party
Rye & Wheat Flatbread (Flatbrød)
Pea Soup with Pork (Ärter med Fläsk)
Rye-Meal Bread (Ruisleipä), page 134, Cheese
Sliced Tomatoes & Butter Lettuce
Apple Pie (Eplepai), Whipped Cream
Fruit-Juice Glögg (Saft Glögg), page 88
Beer Punch (Mumma)

Potato Flatbread

Lefse—Norway

Norwegians serve lefse for all special occasions, including a Coffeetable, page 145.

2 lbs. (5 to 6 large) potatoes, peeled, diced
1 teaspoon salt

2 tablespoons butter
1-1/2 to 2 cups all-purpose flour

In a medium saucepan over medium heat, cook potatoes in water to cover until tender but not mushy, about 20 minutes. Drain, reserving potato water for bread or soup. Press cooked potatoes through potato ricer or grater. There will be about 3-1/3 cups riced or grated potatoes. In a large bowl, combine potatoes, salt and butter. Cool to room temperature. Stir in 1-1/2 cups flour, then stir in enough of remaining flour to make a stiff dough. Divide into 4 portions. Divide each portion into 4 equal pieces, making 16 pieces. Preheat a griddle to 400F (205C). On a lightly floured board, roll 1 piece of dough at a time to a paper-thin 10- or 11-inch circle. Use a grooved *lefse rolling pin,* page 7, to get authentic grid-like texture. Bake dough circle on preheated griddle, 1 to 2 minutes on each side until browned in spots. Lefse will look dry, but will be flexible, not crisp. Fold in half, then in half again. Stack on a piece of waxed paper as they are baked. Repeat with remaining pieces of dough. To serve, unfold and spread with butter. To freeze, wrap airtight; store in freezer. Thaw in wrapper. Makes 16 lefse.

Rye & Wheat Flatbread   Photo on pages 110-111.

Flatbrød—Scandinavia

Serve these oven-baked crackers with cheese or other spreads.

1-1/2 cups boiling water
2 tablespoons butter
1/2 teaspoon salt

1 cup stirred rye flour
1 cup all-purpose flour
1 cup whole-wheat flour

Preheat oven to 450F (230C). In a large bowl, combine water, butter, salt, rye flour and all-purpose flour. Beat well. Stir in whole-wheat flour until smooth and resembles baking-powder-biscuit dough. Divide dough into 4 portions. Cut each portion into quarters. On a generously floured board, roll out each piece of dough to make a thin 10- to 12-inch circle. If desired, use a *hardtack* or *lefse rolling pin,* page 7, to make a pattern on dough. Place 2 or 3 dough circles on an ungreased baking sheet. Bake in preheated oven 3 to 5 minutes or until crisp but not completely browned. Cool baked breads on a rack. Stack 6 completely cooled breads together; wrap airtight. Store in a cool dry place. To serve, break into pieces. Makes 16 breads.

 Pearl sugar is available in food shops that have Scandinavian ingredients and in some cake decorating stores. It is imported from Sweden and is usually sold in one-pound or smaller bags. If you cannot find pearl sugar, substitute crushed sugar cubes or loaf sugar.

Pea Soup with Pork

Ärter med Fläsk—Sweden

After a frolic in the cold winter air, this is the perfect soup to serve—with pork sandwiches.

2 cups dry yellow Swedish peas
3 qts. water
1 (2- to 3-lb.) fresh pork-shoulder roast
3 medium onions, sliced
1/2 teaspoon ground ginger

1/4 teaspoon whole allspice
1 teaspoon dried leaf marjoram
1 teaspoon salt or to taste
1/8 teaspoon ground black pepper

Sort and wash peas. In a deep soup kettle, combine peas and water. Soak overnight. Place soup kettle with soaked peas and water over medium-high heat. Bring to a boil. Remove shells of peas that float to top of water. Simmer 2 hours or until peas are partially softened. Add pork roast, onions, ginger and allspice. Simmer 2 to 3 hours until pork is tender. Skim fat from surface. Stir in marjoram, salt and pepper. To serve, place pork roast on a platter; cut into slices, removing bone. Serve pork in sandwiches, if desired. Serve hot soup in bowls or mugs. Makes 6 servings.

Apple Pie

Eplepai—Norway

For a real treat, serve this fresh from the oven, topped with a dollop of whipped cream.

1 egg
3/4 cup sugar
1 teaspoon vanilla extract
1 teaspoon baking powder
1/4 teaspoon salt

1 teaspoon ground cinnamon
1/2 cup all-purpose flour
1/2 cup chopped pecans or walnuts
2 small, tart apples, diced (about 1 cup)
Whipped cream or cinnamon ice cream

Generously butter a 9-inch pie pan; set aside. Preheat oven to 350F (175C). In a large bowl, combine all ingredients except whipped cream or ice cream. Stir until blended; mixture will be stiff. Spoon into prepared pie pan. Bake 30 minutes or until browned and slightly puffed. To serve, cut hot pie into wedges; top with dollops of whipped cream or ice cream. Makes 6 to 8 servings.

Beer Punch

Mumma—Sweden

This is exceptionally good when you use Scandinavian or German beer.

1 (12-oz.) bottle dark beer
1 (12-oz.) bottle light beer

1 (12-oz.) bottle pale ale
1/4 cup aquavit or gin

Refrigerate all ingredients until chilled. To serve, pour all ingredients into a chilled pitcher; stir. Serve in mugs. Makes 6 servings.

Pea Soup with Pork; Pork sandwich on Country Oat Loaf, page 136; Beer Punch.

❖ Supper at Grandma's Farm ❖

Down-home Scandinavian cooking is usually simple, hearty and nutritious. The recipes in this menu illustrate techniques that Scandinavian cooks have learned and passed down for generations. For instance, a Norwegian grandmother has taught her daughters and granddaughters how to make the lightest-textured, tenderest meat loaf imaginable. The secret lies in beating the meat mixture vigorously—just as carefully as you beat the eggs for a sponge cake.

Norwegians are masters at long, slow simmering. This technique is used to make *Dravle* or Caramel Pudding. The milk is boiled gently until it becomes a slightly sweet, caramel-flavored concentrate. It is delicious with the addition of walnuts. However, nuts aren't traditional.

Famous Norwegian *gjetost* cheese is another example of long, slow simmering. In other countries, the *whey,* or fluid left after making cheese, is usually fed to cattle. In Norway, it is cooked down until it forms a caramel-flavored thick paste, which cools to a solid, tan cheese. *Ekte gjetost* is made with 100% goat's-milk whey. It is in much smaller supply than regular gjetost, a mixture of 10% goat's-milk whey and 90% cow's-milk whey.

Another Norwegian cheese, *gammelost,* or *old cheese,* is made from skim milk. Old-timers insist they owe their present good health and strength to gammelost. It is low in calories and fat and very high in protein—and very aromatic. To eat gammelost, generously spread butter over a piece of dark bread, then top with a thin shaving of gammelost. Nibble slowly.

Recipes are handed down from generation to generation with slight variations as the spirit and available ingredients dictate. The recipe for Potato Dumplings, rich with hearty flavor, has been handed down for at least six generations in one Norwegian family.

From this menu, choose one of the main dishes to serve with the dumplings.

Supper at Grandma's Farm
Grandma Norland's Meat Loaf (Kjøttpudding)
Summer-House Pork Chops (Sommer Koteletter)
Cabbage Rolls (Kåldomar)
Potato Dumplings (Kumle), Apple Slaw (Æblesalat)
Carrot Casserole (Porkkanalaatikko), page 118
Caramel Pudding (Dravle)
Milk, Buttermilk, Coffee, Tea

Grandma Norland's Meat Loaf

Kjøttpudding—Norway

This meatloaf makes excellent cold sandwiches.

2 lbs. lean ground beef
1 lb. lean ground pork
1 cup milk
1 tablespoon all-purpose flour
1 egg

1 small onion, minced
2-1/2 teaspoons salt
1/2 teaspoon pepper
1/2 teaspoon ground allspice

Butter a 9" x 5" loaf pan; set aside. Preheat oven to 325F (165C). In large bowl of electric mixer, combine beef, pork, milk, flour and egg. Beat at low speed until blended, then on high speed 10 minutes or until light and fluffy. Using a wooden spoon, stir in onion, salt, pepper and allspice. Spoon mixture into prepared pan. Bake 1-1/2 hours or until loaf shrinks away from sides of pan. Makes 8 servings.

Summer-House Pork Chops

Sommer Koteletter—Denmark

Combined aromas and flavors of apples, onions and curry powder are wonderful.

1 tablespoon butter
4 pork loin chops, 1 inch thick
3 tart apples, peeled, cored, sliced
1 large onion, diced
1 teaspoon salt

1 teaspoon sugar
1/4 teaspoon black pepper
1 teaspoon curry powder
1 tablespoon butter, melted
1/3 cup dry breadcrumbs

Preheat oven to 350F (175C). Melt 1 tablespoon butter in a large ovenproof skillet over medium heat. Brown pork chops in butter, 3 to 5 minutes on each side. Remove pork chops from skillet. Add apples, onion, salt, sugar, pepper and curry powder to skillet. Arrange browned chops over apple layer. Cover and bake 30 minutes or until chops are tender and apple layer is cooked through. In a small bowl, stir melted butter into breadcrumbs. Sprinkle over baked pork chops. Bake, uncovered, 5 to 10 minutes longer or until crumbs are crisp and browned. Makes 4 servings.

Apple Slaw   Photo on pages 46-47.

AEblesalat—Denmark

Slaw with fruit in it is a Scandinavian favorite.

1/2 cup whipping cream
1/2 cup mayonnaise
1 tablespoon sugar

1 large Red Delicious or Winesap apple
4 cups finely shredded cabbage
1 (8-oz.) can crushed pineapple, drained

In a large bowl, combine cream, mayonnaise and sugar. Core apple; dice but do not peel. Add diced apple and cabbage to mayonnaise mixture. Fold in pineapple. Refrigerate until ready to serve. Makes 8 servings.

Potato Dumplings

Kumle—Norway

Every Norwegian cook has her own favorite version of potato dumplings.

4 cups shredded raw potatoes	16 (1/2-inch) cubes cooked ham
2 cups all-purpose flour	Melted butter
1 tablespoon salt	Chopped parsley
2 to 3 qts. beef, ham or chicken broth	

Place potatoes in a strainer. Rinse with cold water to prevent browning; drain well. In a large bowl, combine flour and salt. Add drained potatoes; stir until potatoes are coated. In a deep medium saucepan, bring broth to a boil over medium heat. Using a serving spoon, scoop a rounded spoonful of potato mixture, about the size of a large egg. Press 1 cube of ham into center, covering completely. Using a slotted spoon, carefully lower dumpling into hot broth. Quickly shape remaining dumplings with ham cubes in center and lower into hot broth. Adjust heat to maintain a simmer but not a hard boil. Simmer at least 45 minutes, turning dumplings over after about 25 minutes. Use a slotted spoon to lift cooked dumplings from hot broth. Serve hot dumplings as a vegetable dish with melted butter. Garnish with chopped parsley. Or, serve with broth, or in broth as a soup. Makes about 16 dumplings or 6 to 8 servings.

Cabbage Rolls

Kåldomar—Scandinavian

A favorite in all of the Scandinavian countries.

2 to 3 qts. boiling water	1 egg
1 large head cabbage	2 teaspoons salt
1 lb. lean ground beef	1/2 teaspoon ground allspice
1 lb. lean ground pork	1 cup milk
1-1/2 cups soft breadcrumbs	2 tablespoons butter, melted
1 small onion, minced	1/2 cup whipping cream

Preheat oven to 300F (150C). Butter a 13" x 9" baking pan; set aside. Remove 16 unblemished large outer leaves from cabbage. Cook leaves in boiling water 1 minute or until softened. Or, place head of cabbage in water. After 1 minute, drain. Remove 16 outer leaves from cabbage. Reserve remaining cabbage for another use. Drain softened leaves on paper towels. In large bowl of electric mixer, combine beef, pork, breadcrumbs, onion, egg, salt, allspice and milk. Beat with electric mixer on high speed until mixture is light and fluffy, about 10 minutes. Divide meat mixture among cabbage leaves, placing an egg-shaped mound near stem-end of each leaf. Roll into bundles, folding sides of cabbage leaves over meat mixture. Arrange cabbage rolls close together, in prepared baking pan, with loose end of leaf on bottom. Brush rolls with melted butter. Bake 1 hour. Drain juices from pan into a large skillet. Over high heat, bring juices to a rolling boil; boil until reduced to make a shiny glaze. Slowly stir cream into glaze. Bring to a boil again. Stirring occasionally, cook until thickened. Arrange cooked cabbage rolls in a shallow bowl. Pour sauce over cabbage rolls. Serve hot. Makes 8 servings or 16 cabbage rolls.

How to Make Potato Dumplings

1/Press a ham cube into center of potato mixture, covering completely.

2/Use a slotted spoon to remove dumplings from hot broth. Sprinkle with butter and parsley.

Caramel Pudding

Dravle—Norway

Milk-sugar caramelizes during long slow cooking to flavor this dessert.

2 qts. homogenized whole milk
2 eggs, slightly beaten
1 cup dairy sour cream

1 tablespoon all-purpose flour
1/2 cup sugar
1/2 cup chopped walnuts

Pour milk into a heavy 4-quart saucepan. Stirring constantly, bring to a boil over medium-low heat. Reduce heat to lowest possible setting. Stirring occasionally, simmer 3 to 4 hours or until milk is reduced to about 4 cups and has a light tan color. In a small bowl, blend eggs, sour cream, flour and sugar. Stir 1/2 cup hot milk into egg mixture. Stir egg mixture into remaining hot milk. Cook and stir over low heat until mixture is thickened and slightly curdled, about 10 minutes. Serve hot, sprinkled with walnuts. Makes 8 servings.

HOLIDAYS

❖ Easter Festival ❖

Easter in Scandinavia is a festival of sun, snow and skiing. Norwegians head for the mountains and observe Easter in a mountain *hytta,* or private hideaway, spending as many hours as possible ski-touring long distances. Finns, Swedes and Danes take the long weekend to head for snowy slopes, if not to Lapland, then to other places in Europe.

Before Easter, the open markets across Scandinavia are filled with arrangements of brilliantly colored chicken feathers tied to leafy birch twigs. The birch twigs are clipped from branches two to three weeks earlier and placed in water to force the green leaves to open. Leafy branches are used to decorate homes. The weather is still cold and there are no flowers blooming, so the dyed chicken feathers make a colorful substitute.

On an Easter visit to relatives in Western Finland, we saw Easter-Saturday bonfires in the field across from the house, set to scare away "witches." Answering a knock on the door, we found two little girls, faces blackened with soot, dressed in witches costumes. Each carried a broomstick with a copper coffeepot hung on the end. Witches, of course, love hot black coffee. Our Great Aunt Lilja stuffed chocolates and Easter eggs into the pots. Then, the little "witches" flew off to the neighbors. We spent the evening witnessing a procession of witches and other scary creatures—despite bonfires!

Although there are no traditional Scandinavian Easter foods, there are regional favorites. Swedes and Norwegians always include fish in the menu. Norwegians like chicken as a main course, even though it is quite expensive in Scandinavia. In all countries, pork and lamb dishes are popular.

Finland has a traditional dessert called *mämmi.* This almost black pudding is made of rye, malt and molasses, and baked in a birchbark basket. Mämmi is a food for which one must acquire a taste. Eastern Finland celebrates Easter with a cheesecake-like dessert called *Pasha.* It is generally served alone, but we suggest a wonderful musk-flavored cloudberry sauce. Scandinavian specialty shops often carry cloudberry preserves.

Easter Festival

Fruit Soup (Fruktsuppe)
Caviar & Potato Slices (Kaviar med Kartoffler)
Crown Roast of Pork Piquant (Svinekam)
Bergen Easter Chicken (Stekt Påske Kylling)
Tomato Salad (Tomatsallad)
Glazed Mushrooms (Glaserede Champignon)
Brussels Sprouts
Finnish Cheesecake (Pasha)
Schnapps, Beer, Milk, Buttermilk, Coffee
Red-Currant Juice, White or Red Wine

Crown Roast of Pork Piquant, filled with Brussels sprouts; Glazed Mushrooms; Caviar & Potato Slices, all on page 40.

Crown Roast of Pork Piquant   Photo on page 39.

Svinekam—Denmark

The mustard glaze gives this pork roast a special flavor.

1/2 cup Dijon-style mustard
2 tablespoons grated fresh horseradish
2 teaspoons anchovy paste

2 tablespoons brown sugar
1 (16-rib, 8-lb.) crown roast of pork
1 cup fine dry breadcrumbs

Preheat oven to 325F (165C). In a small bowl, combine mustard, horseradish, anchovy paste and brown sugar. Place pork roast on a rack in a large roasting pan. Place an inverted metal measuring cup, empty can or glass in center of roast to maintain shape. Brush mustard mixture on all sides of meat. Coat evenly with breadcrumbs. Insert meat thermometer into thickest part of roast, not touching bone. Bake until thermometer registers 180F (80C), 35 to 40 minutes per pound. Let stand 20 minutes before carving. Remove cup, can or glass from center. Carve roast and serve on a round platter. Makes 16 servings.

Glazed Mushrooms   Photo on page 39.

Glaserede Champignon—Denmark

Danes are known for marvelous combinations such as this one.

1 lb. whole small mushrooms
1/4 cup olive oil or vegetable oil
1/2 teaspoon salt
1/2 teaspoon paprika
1 garlic clove, crushed

1 small green onion, chopped
3 tablespoons chopped parsley
1 tablespoon chopped fresh dill, if desired
2 teaspoons dried leaf basil

Clean mushrooms. Remove stems; reserve for another use. Heat oil in a large skillet over medium heat. Stir in salt, paprika, garlic and green onion. Increase heat to high. Add mushrooms; sauté until mushrooms are glazed and coated with oil mixture, 3 to 5 minutes. Top with parsley, dill, if desired and basil; toss lightly. Serve immediately. Makes 8 servings.

Caviar & Potato Slices   Photo on page 39.

Kaviar med Kartoffler—Denmark

This is one of the simplest and most impressive hors d'oeuvres!

1/2 cup vegetable oil
4 medium potatoes

1/2 cup dairy sour cream
1 (2-oz.) jar red or black caviar

Preheat oven to 500F (260C). Spread 1/4 cup oil in each of 2 jelly-roll pans. Scrub potatoes thoroughly. Cut potatoes crosswise into 1/4-inch slices; rinse under very cold water to prevent browning. Dry on paper towels. Dip both sides of potato slices in oil in prepared pans, then arrange in pans in a single layer. Bake 10 to 12 minutes or until potatoes are crisp around edges and lightly browned. Drain on paper towels, if desired. Arrange baked potato slices on a platter or tray. Top each with a dollop of sour cream and about 1/4 teaspoon caviar. Serve immediately. Makes about 32 appetizers.

How to Make Crown Roast of Pork Piquant

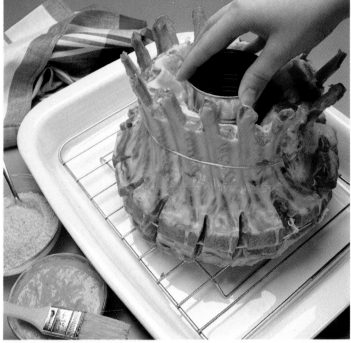

1/Place a custard cup or can in center of crown roast to hold shape during baking.

2/Insert a meat thermometer into thickest part of roast, not touching bone.

Bergen Easter Chicken

Stekt Påske Kylling—Norway

Gjetost, the caramel-colored whey cheese of Norway, adds color and richness to the sauce.

1 (3-lb.) broiler-fryer chicken, cut up
1 teaspoon salt
1/2 teaspoon ground white pepper
2 tablespoons butter
1 cup chicken broth or water
1/4 cup sherry or
   2 tablespoons lemon juice

1/4 cup chopped fresh parsley
1/2 cup whipping cream
1 cup shredded gjetost or
   aged Cheddar cheese (4 oz.)
Chopped fresh parsley for garnish

Remove skin from chicken; rub meat with salt and pepper. Melt butter in a large skillet over medium heat. Add chicken; brown on all sides. Pour broth or water over browned chicken. Add sherry or lemon juice. Cover; reduce heat to low. Simmer 35 to 45 minutes or until chicken is tender. Use a slotted spoon to place cooked chicken on a platter; keep warm. Add 1/4 cup chopped parsley and cream to drippings in pan. Stirring constantly, bring to a simmer. Cook and stir until sauce is reduced to about 1 cup and has a glazed appearance. Stir in cheese only until melted. Pour sauce over chicken. Garnish with fresh parsley. Makes 4 servings.

Tomato Salad

Tomatisallad—Sweden

Tomatoes and cucumbers are popular in Sweden.

6 medium tomatoes
Boiling water
4 green onions with tops, sliced
2 tablespoons red- or white-wine vinegar
1 tablespoon sugar
1/2 teaspoon crushed whole allspice

1/4 teaspoon ground white pepper
2 teaspoons salt
1/4 cup vegetable oil
1 (8-inch) European-style or
    other cucumber, sliced paper-thin
Chopped fresh parsley for garnish

Immerse tomatoes in boiling water, about 15 seconds. Immerse in cold water, then quickly core and peel. Cut peeled tomatoes into thin slices; arrange on a 2-inch-deep platter. Sprinkle with green onions. In a small bowl, whisk together vinegar, sugar, allspice, white pepper and 1 teaspoon salt. Slowly beat in oil with a whisk until blended. Pour over tomatoes. Drain cucumbers on paper towels; sprinkle with remaining teaspoon salt. Pat dry with paper towels. Loosely pile cucumbers in a mound on center of platter over tomato slices. Sprinkle with parsley. Serve immediately or refrigerate up to 6 hours before serving. Makes 8 to 10 servings.

Finnish Cheesecake

Pasha—Finland

Traditionally, this is served plain, but we prefer the variation given below.

2 qts. dairy buttermilk
1 egg
1 cup dairy sour cream
1/2 cup sugar

1/2 cup ground almonds
1/2 cup butter
1/2 teaspoon vanilla extract

Pour buttermilk into a 3-quart casserole dish. Cover and place in oven. Begin heating oven to 250F (120C). Also begin timing; bake 3 hours. Line a large sieve with several layers of cheesecloth or paper towels. Place lined sieve over a large, deep bowl. Pour mixture into lined sieve; let drain overnight. Discard whey or save for another use. Pour curd from lined sieve into a large bowl. Beat in egg, then sour cream, sugar and almonds. Melt butter in a heavy, large saucepan. Stir curd mixture into melted butter. Attach a candy thermometer to side of pan with bulb in curd mixture. Stir mixture over medium heat until thermometer reaches 190F to 200F (90C to 95C). Do not scorch. Stir in vanilla. Line a wooden cheese mold or an unglazed clay flowerpot with a double thickness of cheesecloth. Place mold in a medium bowl. Spoon mixture into mold; fold edges of cheesecloth over top of curd mixture. Press down to compact mixture. Place a small plate or saucer on top of mixture, then place a weight on top. Refrigerate 2 to 3 days. Remove mold from bowl; pull back folded cheesecloth. Invert mold onto a plate. Remove mold and cheesecloth. To serve, cut into 1/2-inch horizontal slices. Makes 8 servings.

Variation

Blend 1 cup cloudberry or raspberry preserves with 1/4 cup orange juice or orange-flavored liqueur. Spoon a small amount onto each plate, then top with a slice of Finnish Cheesecake.

❖ Christmas Eve Supper ❖

In Sweden, Santa Claus is a *Tomte,* or gnome—a tiny little fellow who lives somewhere among the outbuildings. Father or an uncle or neighbor dresses up as the Christmas Tomte to hand out gifts. He is a bit on the large side, but the children don't seem to notice.

In Denmark, they begin celebrating Christmas on the first day of December. *Julenisse,* the Danish counterpart of the Swedish Tomte, delivers a gift to the children every day for 23 days!

In Scandinavia, the Christmas tree is never in place until Christmas Eve. In Denmark, this is a dramatic affair. Adults decorate the tree with handmade ornaments—angels, birds, apples, hearts, cookies—and real candles. The children are not allowed to see the tree until the candles are lit. As they enter the room with the youngest child leading the way, everyone joins hands and circles the tree, singing Christmas carols. They sing at least ten Christmas carols, then open gifts.

In Norway, church bells begin ringing at 4:00 p.m. on Christmas Eve. The bells are a signal that Christmas is beginning. After church, the children go on a *julebukke* round, visiting the homes of relatives and friends where they are treated to Christmas cookies and other goodies. At home, the tree is being trimmed, and the mysterious little Julenisse makes his way down each chimney and delivers gifts.

When the children arrive at home, the family has a light supper or a full smörgåsbord. After supper, the family sings and dances around the Christmas tree. The lucky person who got an almond in his or her rice pudding is usually named the Julenisse for the evening and gets to distribute the gifts.

Christmas traditions vary among families. For many, Christmas Eve is the time for a big, traditional dinner or smörgåsbord. For others, supper may simply be rice pudding—nothing else. Or it may be *lutfisk,* meatballs and rice pudding. Meatballs are always served as an alternative for those who do not like lutfisk.

In Finland, large pots of tar are burned on either side of the entrance to the church to commemorate those who lost their lives in wars for independence. Candles are lit and placed on graves throughout the cemetary that surrounds the church. On Christmas Eve, the night is black and snow covers the ground in deep drifts, making the scene one of awe and beauty.

After supper, *Joulupukki,* or Santa Claus, warmly dressed in a long red coat, pointed leather boots, a warm red wool cap and thick mittens, knocks at the door. He asks the children if they have been good and to prove it by singing a song. The children, wearing red pointed *tonttu,* or gnome hats, nervously, but obediently, sing. Joulupukki praises them profusely, then distributes gifts.

Christmas Eve Supper

Christmas Cod (Lutfisk), White Sauce (Vit Sås)
Swedish Meatballs (Köttbullar)
Dilled Green Peas (Tilliherneet), Boiled Potatoes
Potato Flatbread (Lefse), page 124
Finnish Rice Pudding (Riisipuuro)
Milk, Coffee, Fruit-Juice Glögg (Saft Glögg), page 88

Christmas Cod

Lutfisk—Sweden

Ready-to-cook lutfisk can be purchased in specialty stores, gourmet stores and supermarkets.

4 lbs. lutfisk or cod
Boiling water
1 teaspoon salt
1/4 teaspoon ground white pepper

1/4 teaspoon ground allspice
1/2 cup butter, melted
White Sauce, below

Remove skin from fish. Bones are large enough to remove easily after fish is served. Place fish in a deep pot; cover with boiling water. Bring to a simmer over medium-low heat; do not boil. Simmer 10 to 15 minutes or until fish flakes easily, quivers like jelly and becomes translucent. Drain fish; place on a hot platter. Sprinkle with salt, white pepper and allspice. Drizzle melted butter over fish. Serve with White Sauce. Makes 4 to 6 servings.

White Sauce

Vit Sås—Sweden

The secret to a smooth sauce is to stir constantly.

1/4 cup butter
1/4 cup all-purpose flour
1-1/2 cups milk

1 teaspoon salt
1/4 teaspoon ground allspice or white pepper

Melt butter in a medium saucepan over medium heat. Stir in flour. Slowly stir in milk. Stirring constantly, cook until sauce is thickened and smooth. Stir in salt and allspice or white pepper. Serve hot. Makes about 2 cups.

Dilled Green Peas

Tilliherneet—Finland

Green peas, seasoned with dill and topped with cheese—absolutely delicious!

2 (10-oz.) pkgs. frozen green peas
2 tablespoons butter
2 tablespoons chopped shallots or
   green onions

1 teaspoon dried dill weed
2 tablespoons chopped pimiento
1 cup shredded Jarlsberg cheese (4 oz.)

Cook peas as package directs. Melt butter in a small skillet over medium heat. Add shallots or green onions; sauté 2 minutes or until soft. Stir in hot cooked peas, dill and pimiento. Pour into a serving dish; sprinkle cheese over top. Serve immediately. Makes 6 servings.

Swedish Meatballs

Köttbullar—Sweden

Serve meatballs as an alternative main dish for those who don't care for Lutfisk, opposite.

1-1/2 cups soft breadcrumbs
1 cup half and half
1 tablespoon butter
1/2 cup chopped onion
1 lb. lean ground beef
1/2 lb. lean ground pork
1 egg
1/4 cup minced fresh parsley

1-1/2 teaspoons salt
1/2 teaspoon ground ginger
1/2 teaspoon ground allspice
1/2 teaspoon ground nutmeg
2 tablespoons butter
2 tablespoons all-purpose flour
2 cups beef broth

In large bowl of electric mixer, soak breadcrumbs in half and half, 10 minutes. Melt 1 tablespoon butter in a large skillet over medium heat. Add onion; sauté until soft, about 3 minutes. Stir into breadcrumb mixture. Add beef, pork, egg, parsley, salt, ginger, allspice and nutmeg. With electric mixer, beat at high speed until mixture is fluffy. Dip 2 teaspoons in ice water until cold. Use cold spoons to shape meat mixture into tiny meatballs. Melt 2 tablespoons butter in skillet used to sauté onion. Brown meatballs in butter, turning to brown evenly on all sides. Drain cooked meatballs on paper towels. Stir flour into drippings in skillet. Gradually whisk in broth. Continue stirring until mixture thickens. Return meatballs to sauce in skillet. Simmer 15 minutes or until meatballs are heated through. Makes 4 to 6 servings or about 48 meatballs.

Finnish Rice Pudding

Riisipuuro—Finland

All Scandinavian countries claim this creamy rice pudding as their own.

1/2 cup sugar
1 tablespoon ground cinnamon
3/4 cup medium-grain rice, uncooked
3/4 cup water
2 tablespoons butter
4 cups milk
1 teaspoon salt

1 (3-inch) cinnamon stick
1/4 teaspoon ground nutmeg
1 teaspoon grated lemon peel
1 teaspoon vanilla extract
1 whole almond, shelled, blanched
About 1/4 cup butter, melted

In a small bowl, combine sugar and 1 tablespoon cinnamon; set aside. In a large saucepan, combine rice and water. Bring to boil over medium-high heat. Stir in 2 tablespoons butter, milk, salt and cinnamon stick. Stirring occasionally, simmer over low heat, uncovered, until thickened, about 35 minutes. Remove cinnamon stick; stir in nutmeg, lemon peel and vanilla. To serve, stir almond into pudding; spoon pudding into individual dessert dishes. Sprinkle top of each serving with cinnamon-sugar mixture. Spoon melted butter over each. Serve hot. Makes 6 servings.

Clockwise from lower left: Rye Dipping Bread, page 134; Dip-in-the-Kettle Soup, page 50; Apple Slaw, page 35; Butter-Cookie Shells, page 151; Spicy Christmas Pigs, page 147; Krumbcakes, page 150; Marinated Oranges, page 54; Rutabaga-Potato Casserole, page 115. Center: Home-Cured Christmas Ham, page 51.

Old-Fashioned
❖ Christmas Smörgåsbord ❖

Early in December in old Scandinavia, feverish preparations for Christmas began. Pressed-meat dishes had to be prepared and preserved—but were not tasted until Christmas Eve or Christmas day. Most important was the home-preserved ham. Its preparation was started during the first week of Advent, after the slaughtering of the *house pig.*

In the old days, every household had a special pig that was fed all the best table scraps throughout the year. It was named the *talous porsus* in Finland. Today, a family member who willing cleans up the last bits of a meal, may lovingly be called the talous porsus. As could be expected, the house pig became a family pet. It was difficult to face the slaughtering, much less the eating of a pet, so families often exchanged animals.

The best ham was selected for the Christmas meal. It was brined, then smoked, if the farm had a smoke sauna. After two weeks of curing, the ham was baked in a rye crust. The good, rich broth in the baking pan tempted the family into the kitchen at about 2:00 p.m. on Christmas Eve to take part in a yearly ritual called *dip-in-the-kettle* or *doppa i grytan.* Everyone dipped a piece of bread, or the rye crust in which the ham was baked, into the steaming broth. After the crust was removed from the ham, the ham was coated with a mustard-crumb-sugar mixture and browned, in preparation for the big meal.

In our menu, we have made the dip-in-the-kettle custom the first-course serving of soup and bread. Serve the soup in bowls at the table or in mugs as a stand-up course. If you have a kitchen ceremony, as in olden days, let family members dip slices of buttered rye bread into the broth. Then, on a plate, serve a slice of the ham or some Christmas sausages. This little snack probably took the place of a midday meal on Christmas Eve because of the large evening smörgåsbord to follow.

To Swedish families, the aroma of the *Jul* ham baking the night before Christmas Eve, is as important as the remaining holiday festivities. The traditional ham is large enough to last the entire holiday and is enjoyed for sandwiches and snacking after the main Christmas meal has been served.

Pickled herring, in many varieties, are always part of a smörgåsbord. Pickled herring are available in Scandinavian specialty shops or by mail, page 154. Marinated Anchovies calls for Swedish anchovies as the main ingredient. Don't confuse *Swedish* anchovies with more salty *Portuguese* anchovies.

Let guests serve themselves from this smörgåsbord. First, serve Dip-in-the-Kettle Soup. Next, suggest they sample the herring dishes. For the third course, give them clean plates and have them sample the cold-meat dishes that were prepared weeks before Christmas. The main course, Home-Cured Christmas Ham, requires another clean dish. Serve a salad or a choice of salads. Boiled potatoes are always included. Giving guests another clean plate, serve a variety of puddings or other desserts. Serve any or all of the selections buffet-style.

Many families serve a meal similar to this one on Christmas Day, and on Christmas Eve have a simple supper of Christmas Cod, page 44.

Old-Fashioned Christmas Smörgåsbord

First Course:
Dip-in-the-Kettle Soup (Doppa i Grytan)
Rye Dipping Bread (Doppbröd), page 134

Fish Course:
Marinated Anchovies (Marinerad Ansjovis)
Mustard Herring (Senapsill)

Cold-Meat Course:
Veal Terrine (Sylte), page 8
Pressed-Beef Roll (Rullepulse), Pressed-Pork Roll (Käärysyltty)

Hot-Food Course:
Home-Cured Christmas Ham (Julskinka)
Baked Mushrooms (Paistettu Sienet), Boiled Potatoes

Salad Course:
Christmas Salad (Julsallad), Winter Salad (Vintersallad)
Marinated Oranges (Marinerte Appelsiner)

Dessert Course:
Christmas Rice Pudding (Julgrøt)
Norwegian Cream Pudding (Rømmegrøt)
Danish Pastries, pages 138 to 144
Cookies, pages 146 to 154

Fruit-Juice Glögg (Saft Glögg), page 88
Hot Wine Punch (Glögg), page 109, Beer, Milk

Baked Mushrooms

Paistettu Sienet — Finland

Mushrooms, especially wild ones, appear often in Finnish meals.

1/4 cup butter	2 tablespoons all-purpose flour
2 lbs. mushrooms, quartered	1/2 cup water
1 green onion, chopped	1/2 cup whipping cream
1/2 teaspoon salt	1/4 cup soft breadcrumbs
1/4 teaspoon freshly ground black pepper	

Preheat oven to 450F (230C). Butter a shallow 2-quart baking dish; set aside. Melt butter in a large skillet. Add mushrooms and green onion; stirring occasionally, sauté 5 minutes over high heat. Sprinkle with salt, pepper and flour; stir to blend. Pour mushroom mixture into prepared baking dish; set aside. Pour water into skillet. Bring to a boil over high heat; stir until drippings are blended to make a sauce. Pour over mushrooms. Pour whipping cream over mushrooms. Sprinkle with breadcrumbs. Bake 10 minutes or until bubbly. Makes 8 servings.

Dip-in-the-Kettle Soup   Photo on pages 46-47.

Doppa i Grytan — Sweden

Serve this thin, savory soup as a first course for Christmas dinner.

**6 cups ham or roast-beef broth
   or canned broth
Salt and pepper to taste**

**Rye Dipping Bread, page 134, torn in pieces
2 tablespoons butter, melted
3 or 4 thin lemon slices**

Pour broth into a large saucepan. Add salt and pepper to taste. Bring to a boil over medium heat. Toast bread in broiler. Sprinkle with butter. Pour hot broth into a soup tureen. Garnish with lemon slices. To serve, place pieces of toasted bread in 6 individual soup bowls. Pour broth over bread. Serve immediately. Makes 6 servings.

Marinated Anchovies

Marinerad Ansjovis — Sweden

Do not use Portuguese anchovies that are smaller, saltier and drier than Swedish anchovies.

**1 (3- or 3-1/2-oz.) can Swedish
   anchovy fillets
3 tablespoons vegetable oil
1 tablespoon white-wine vinegar**

**1/8 teaspoon paprika
2 tablespoons thinly sliced green onion,
   with tops**

Drain anchovies. Roll up fillets and arrange in rows in a small serving dish. In a small bowl, combine oil, vinegar and paprika. Beat with a whisk. Pour over anchovies. Sprinkle with onion. Cover and refrigerate 2 or more hours. Baste occasionally to keep anchovies moist. Makes 12 or 13 marinated fillets.

Mustard Herring

Senapsill — Sweden

Purchase herring fillets in wine sauce from a specialty shop, supermarket, or by mail, page 154.

**1 (16-oz.) jar herring fillets in wine sauce
3 egg yolks
1 tablespoon prepared Swedish- or
   German-style mustard
1 tablespoon red-wine vinegar**

**1/2 teaspoon salt
1/4 teaspoon ground white pepper
1 teaspoon sugar
1 cup vegetable oil
1/4 cup dried dill weed, crumbled**

Drain herring; place in a medium bowl. In a small bowl, combine egg yolks, mustard, vinegar, salt, white pepper and sugar. Use a whisk to gradually beat in oil until mixture is thick and creamy. Stir in dill. Pour over herring. Cover and refrigerate 3 to 4 hours. Spoon into a serving bowl. Makes 12 to 16 herring pieces.

Home-Cured Christmas Ham   Photo on pages 46-47.

Julskinka—Scandinavia

This home-cured ham will not be as salty as commercially prepared hams.

1 (12- to 14-lb.) fresh leg of pork
2 tablespoons brown sugar
1/2 cup meat-curing salt or
   1/2 cup pickling salt and
   2 tablespoons saltpeter
10 qts. water
8 cups meat-curing salt or
   8 cups pickling salt and
   1 cup saltpeter

About 1-1/2 cups water
6 cups rye flour
4 to 6 small baking apples
1/2 lb. large pitted prunes
Mustard-Crumb Coating, see below
1 small red apple, polished
1 small orange, same size as apple
Royal Icing, see below

Mustard-Crumb Coating:
2 cups fine dry breadcrumbs
1 cup packed brown sugar

1/2 cup prepared mustard
2 teaspoons ground ginger

Royal Icing:
1 egg white
3 cups powdered sugar

Remove skin and most of fat from pork. In a small bowl, combine brown sugar and 1/2 cup curing salt or 1/2 cup pickling salt and 2 tablespoons saltpeter. Rub mixture over entire surface of ham. Place ham in a deep, nonmetal container deep enough to hold ham covered with brine. Brine is added later. Cover and refrigerate 2 days. In a large pot, combine 10 quarts water with 8 cups curing salt or 8 cups pickling salt and 1 cup saltpeter. Bring to a boil over high heat; stir until salt is dissolved. Cool; pour brine over ham. If necessary, add more water to cover ham completely. Refrigerate 10 days. Rinse ham in cold water, using several changes of water; pat dry. Preheat oven to 350F (175C). In a large bowl, stir enough water into rye flour to make a stiff dough. Turn out onto a lightly floured board; knead until smooth. Dough may be sticky. Roll out dough to an 18-inch square or large enough to encase ham. Place ham on dough; fold dough around ham, covering completely. Insert meat thermometer into thickest part of ham, not touching bone. Place ham on a rack in a shallow roasting pan. Bake 5 hours or until thermometer registers 175F (80C). After about 4 hours, place baking apples in a 9-inch square baking pan. Bake 1 hour or until apples are tender, but not broken. Cook prunes as directed on package; cool and drain. Remove crust from baked ham; reserve for dipping, if desired. Prepare Mustard-Crumb Coating. Spread over ham, covering completely. Pat breadcrumb mixture over ham to make an even coating. Bake 10 to 15 minutes or until crumbs are browned and crisp. Press apple onto pointed end of a 6-inch wooden skewer. Press orange onto pointed end of same skewer. Using 1-1/2 yards red ribbon, tie ribbon to blunt end of skewer; set aside. Prepare Royal Icing. Pipe icing in a criss-cross pattern over ham. Place ham on a platter. Garnish with cooked prunes and baked apples. Insert pointed end of skewer into shank end of ham. Serve hot. Makes 25 servings.

Mustard-Crumb Coating:
Blend mustard and ground ginger; set aside. Blend breadcrumbs and brown sugar; set aside.

Royal Icing:
In a small bowl, beat egg white until frothy. Gradually beat in powdered sugar until smooth. Add water if necessary to make a soft icing. Spoon icing into a pastry bag with a thin writing tip.

Pressed-Beef Roll   Photo on pages 110-111.

Rullepulse—Scandinavia

Start three days in advance to make this beef roll with a pork-tenderloin center.

1-1/2 lbs. beef flank steak	1 cup meat-curing salt or 1 cup pickling
1 teaspoon salt	salt and 2 tablespoons saltpeter
1 teaspoon ground allspice	4 cups water
1 small onion, minced	Cold water
1 lb. whole pork tenderloin, fat removed	

Cut 2 pieces of plastic wrap twice as large as flank steak; set aside. Leaving 1 long edge not cut through, use a sharp knife to cut steak horizontally. Or, ask your butcher to *butterfly* steak. Lay meat on 1 piece of plastic wrap, cut-side up. Top with second piece of plastic wrap. With flat side of a meat mallet or cleaver, pound meat until 1/3 to 1/2 inch thick. Remove and discard plastic wrap. Sprinkle flattened meat with 1 teaspoon salt, allspice and onion. Place pork tenderloin on 1 end of meat, parallel to long grain of flank steak. Roll up meat tightly, jelly-roll fashion. Tie firmly with cotton string or, using a darning needle, sew steak to keep it rolled. Place in a nonmetal, 9" x 5" loaf pan. Dissolve meat-curing salt or pickling salt and saltpeter in 4 cups water. Pour over rolled meat. Brine should cover meat. Cover and refrigerate 48 hours. Remove meat from brine; discard brine. Place meat in a deep pot. Add cold water until 4 inches above meat. Bring to a boil; simmer over low heat 3 hours or until meat is tender when pierced with a fork. Add more water, if necessary, to keep meat covered. Lift meat from water; place in nonmetal loaf pan. Add cooking liquid to cover. Cover loosely with plastic wrap. Place a plate or another weight on meat to keep it submerged in cooking liquid. Refrigerate until chilled, about 1 hour. Discard liquid. Meat roll may be wrapped airtight and frozen. Thaw in wrapper in refrigerator for best flavor. Remove string. To serve, cut in 1/4-inch slices. Makes about 30 slices.

Pressed-Pork Roll

Käärysyltty—Finland

Have the butcher "butterfly" a boneless pork loin for you.

1 (4-lb.) boneless pork loin	1/2 teaspoon ground ginger
1/2 teaspoon pepper	6 whole allspice
Boiling water	1 onion, thinly sliced
2 tablespoons salt	1 carrot, thinly sliced

Cut 2 pieces of plastic wrap, twice as large as meat. Lay pork loin on a flat surface. Leaving 1 long edge not cut through, use a sharp knife to cut meat horizontally. This is called *butterflying*. Meat will be about 1 inch thick. Lay meat, cut-side up, between pieces of plastic wrap. With flat side of a meat mallet or cleaver, pound meat until about 1/2 inch thick. Remove and discard plastic wrap. Sprinkle meat with pepper; roll up tightly, jelly-roll fashion, beginning on 1 long side. Tie with cotton string or, using a darning needle, sew meat to keep it rolled. Place rolled meat in a large, deep pot. Add boiling water to cover. Add salt, ginger, allspice, onion and carrot. Bring to a boil. Cover and simmer over low heat 3 hours. Cool meat in broth 30 minutes. Remove meat from broth; place in a nonmetal, 9-inch square dish. Cover with plastic wrap or waxed paper. Place another 9-inch square dish on top of meat. Place several cans of food in top dish. Refrigerate overnight. Meat roll may be wrapped airtight and frozen. Thaw in wrapper in refrigerator for best flavor. Remove string. To serve, cut in 1/4-inch slices. Makes about 30 slices.

How to Make Pressed-Beef Roll

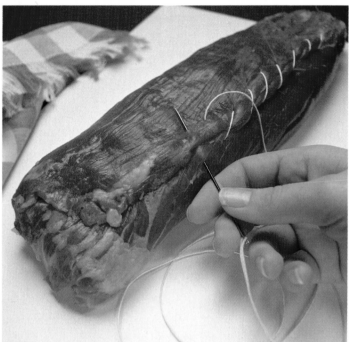

1/Use a sharp knife to cut steak horizontally, leaving 1 long edge attached.

2/Roll pork tenderloin inside steak. Tie with cotton string, or sew to keep rolled.

Christmas Salad

Julsallad—Scandinavia

The fresh flavors in this salad blend and season it without additional spices.

1 large green apple, cored, diced
1 cup finely chopped pickled beets
2 cups finely shredded red cabbage

1 tablespoon lemon juice
Dash salt
Lettuce

In a large bowl, combine apple, beets, cabbage, lemon juice and salt. Cover and refrigerate until chilled. Line a serving plate or platter with lettuce; top with cabbage mixture. Makes 8 servings.

 To determine the volume of a baking dish or mold, pour in water, 1 cup at a time, to within 1/4 inch of the rim.

Winter Salad

Vintersallad—Swedish

This crisp, tangy salad can be prepared in advance.

2 grapefruit
2 heads Belgian endive
2 cups finely shredded white cabbage

2 green onions, thinly sliced
1/3 cup frozen orange-juice concentrate,
  thawed

Section grapefruit by removing peel and all of white portion. Cut on both sides of membranes separating sections. Lift out fruit. Remove and reserve large outer leaves from endive; slice center portion into thin shreds. In a large bowl, combine grapefruit sections, sliced endive, cabbage and green onions. Stir in orange-juice concentrate. Spoon into a medium serving bowl. Tuck reserved outer leaves from endive around edge of salad. Cover and refrigerate 3 to 4 hours before serving. Makes about 8 servings.

Marinated Oranges   Photo on pages 46-47.

Marinerte Appelsiner—Norway

A mild garlic-flavored marinade brings out the subtle flavor of fresh orange slices.

8 seedless oranges
1 garlic clove, minced or pressed
3 tablespoons vegetable oil

1/8 teaspoon white pepper
Minced fresh rosemary for garnish

Peel oranges, removing all of white portion. Cut into 1/3-inch slices. Arrange in an overlapping pattern on a shallow platter. In a small bowl, blend garlic, oil and white pepper. Drizzle over orange slices. Sprinkle with rosemary. Cover and refrigerate 1 hour. Makes 8 servings.

Christmas Rice Pudding

Julgrøt—Scandinavia

There are many versions of this favorite pudding.

3/4 cup medium-grain rice, uncooked
1/2 teaspoon salt
1-1/2 cups boiling water
2 cups whipping cream
2 cups milk
1 (3-inch) cinnamon stick
2 eggs, beaten

1 tablespoon butter
1/3 cup sugar
1/2 teaspoon freshly ground cardamom
1 whole almond, shelled, blanched
1/2 cup sugar
1 tablespoon ground cinnamon
1 to 2 cups half and half

Preheat oven to 325F (165C). Butter a deep 2-quart casserole dish; set aside. In a medium saucepan, combine rice, salt and boiling water. Cover and simmer over low heat 10 minutes. Stir in whipping cream, milk, cinnamon stick, eggs, butter, 1/3 cup sugar, cardamom and almond. Spoon rice mixture into prepared casserole dish. Bake 2 hours or until rice swells and has a creamy texture. In a small bowl, combine 1/2 cup sugar and 1 tablespoon cinnamon. Serve pudding hot or cold with half and half and cinnamon-sugar mixture. Makes 8 to 12 servings.

Norwegian Cream Pudding

Rømmegrøt—Norway

To make this delicious, smooth pudding, purchase the richest cream possible.

2 cups rich whipping cream
1/3 cup all-purpose flour
1-1/2 cups milk
1/2 teaspoon salt

2 tablespoons sugar
1 tablespoon ground cinnamon
1/2 cup sugar

Pour cream into a heavy 3- or 4-quart saucepan; bring to a boil over medium heat. Place flour in a sifter or sieve. While sifting flour into cream, beat with a whisk, keeping mixture smooth. Beat mixture with a wooden spoon as it cooks over low heat. Cook and stir 15 minutes or until mixture is thickened, comes away from side of pan and is reduced in volume. Continue to cook and stir until butterfat separates from flour mixture. Pour butterfat into a small serving dish to serve later. Rich cream will produce at least 1/2 cup butterfat. Slowly stir in milk, salt and 2 tablespoons sugar; heat until mixture comes to a boil. Beat with whisk until smooth. If lumps will not smooth out, pour mixture through a sieve, or process in a blender or food processor until smooth. In a small bowl, stir cinnamon into 1/2 cup sugar. Serve hot pudding in dessert bowls. Serve with rendered butterfat and cinnamon-sugar mixture. Makes 6 to 8 servings.

Note: Ultra-pasteurized cream does not separate during cooking. If your cream does not separate, serve melted Clarified Butter, page 63, with pudding.

How to Make Norwegian Cream Pudding

1/Continue to cook paste mixture until butterfat separates or renders out.

2/Remove butterfat. Whisk in milk, salt and sugar until thick and smooth.

CELEBRATIONS

◈ May Day Brunch Buffet ◈

Welcome spring! When spring arrives, Scandinavia bursts into color and action. Winter is gone and summer is yet to come. May Day eve, or *Walpurgis night*—is celebrated with *fire festivals.* Huge bonfires are set on the highest hill available so they can be seen at great distances. It was an old pagan belief that bonfires and noise would drive away evil spirits, wolves and witches.

In old Sweden, *egg-singing* was a custom practiced on Walpurgis night. Young people would march from farm to farm, stopping outside each home to sing the 28 verses of an old May Day song about the wonders of spring, summer and being young. If they were well-received, the singers would place a green twig on the roof of the house—a symbol of fertility. In return, the farmer paid them with fresh eggs.

Finns are normally quiet, but on the eve of May Day, there is much laughing, singing and partying. It is the time to savor good food and to play old-fashioned games such as *drop the handkerchief,* and to dance around the Maypole.

Both grownups and children carry huge, colorful balloons purchased from sidewalk vendors. Starting on the evening of April 30th, students don white caps and dance, sing and party until the next morning.

May Day is the time to drop in on friends and enjoy their *Sima,* a lemon-flavored beverage made bubbly with yeast. Crisp *Tippaleipä,* similar to funnel cake, is served with Sima. Traditionally, both are served only for May Day. About that time of year, both of these treats are available in coffeeshops in Finland. They are not hard to make. Start the Sima several days in advance to give the flavor time to develop. Tippaleipä is a deep-fried pastry that is best eaten just after frying. Guests can even fry their own. This is a perfect back-porch or patio activity.

The substantial part of your buffet includes ham or another cooked meat and *Ost Låda,* a Swedish Cheese Casserole. Assemble the casserole and refrigerate it overnight. Let it sit at room temperature 30 minutes, before baking.

May Day Brunch Buffet
May Day Crullers (Tippaleipä)
Sliced Cooked Ham
Cheese Casserole (Ost Låda)
Cardamom Coffee Braid (Pulla), page 133
Rye-Meal Bread (Ruisleipä), page 134
Crisp Cheese Sticks (Oststänger)
Lemon Sparkle (Sima), Coffee

Cheese Casserole

Ost Låda—Sweden

Very much like a crustless quiche.

8 Swedish anchovy fillets
2 cups shredded Gouda or
   Jarlsberg cheese (8 oz.)

4 eggs
2 cups half and half
2 tablespoons chopped fresh parsley

Butter a 9- or 10-inch quiche pan or shallow casserole dish. Preheat oven to 350F (175C). Arrange anchovies over bottom of prepared pan or dish. Sprinkle cheese over top. In a medium bowl, beat eggs; stir in half and half. Pour over cheese and anchovies. Bake 25 minutes or until golden brown around edge. Sprinkle with parsley. Serve hot or cool. Makes 6 servings.

Lemon Sparkle

Sima—Finland

Beer adds an authentic malt-like flavor to this refreshing, sparkling drink.

2 lemons
4 qts. water
3 cups packed brown sugar
1 teaspoon active dry yeast

1/4 teaspoon ground ginger
1 (12-oz.) bottle light beer, if desired
8 teaspoons granulated sugar
1 tablespoon raisins

Wash and dry lemons. Use a vegetable peeler to cut yellow zest from peel; set aside. Remove and discard all white pith from lemons. Cut peeled lemons in thin slices. In a 5- to 6-quart saucepan, bring water to a boil over high heat. Stir in brown sugar until dissolved. Add lemon peel and sliced lemons. Remove from heat; cool. Pour into a large nonmetal container. Stir in yeast, ginger and beer, if desired. Cover and let stand at room temperature overnight or until tiny bubbles form around edge. Sterilize pint or quart bottles or a gallon bottle. Scald caps, lids or corks in boiling water. Spoon granulated sugar and a few raisins into each bottle or jar, adding 1 teaspoon sugar for each pint of liquid. Strain liquid before pouring into sterile bottles. Attach sterile caps, lids or corks. Let stand at room temperature until raisins raise to top, 8 hours to 2 days. Refrigerate until ready to serve. Serve cold. Makes about 4 quarts.

Crisp Cheese Sticks

Oststänger—Sweden

Serve these crispy sticks with salads or soups.

1/4 cup butter, room temperature
1/2 cup all-purpose flour
1/2 cup shredded Swiss, Cheddar or
   Edam cheese (2 oz.)

1 to 2 tablespoons water, if necessary
1 egg, beaten
1/4 cup poppy, caraway or sesame seeds

Generously grease a jelly-roll pan; set aside. Preheat oven to 375F (190C). In a small bowl, combine butter, flour and cheese until mixture forms a ball. If needed, stir in 1 to 2 tablespoons water. Refrigerate 20 minutes. On a lightly floured board, roll out dough to a 12" x 10" rectangle. Cut in 4" x 2" strips. Twist strips 2 to 4 times. Dip in beaten egg, then in seeds. Arrange on prepared pan. Bake 8 to 10 minutes until crisp and golden brown. Makes 15 cheese sticks.

How to Make May Day Crullers

1/Squeeze batter through opening into hot oil, swirling in a circular design.

2/Fry until golden brown on both sides. Use a slotted spoon to remove from hot oil.

May Day Crullers

Tippaleipä—Finland

These "bird's nests" are similar to funnel cakes.

1 (1/4-oz.) envelope active dry yeast
2 tablespoons warm water (110F, 45C)
2 eggs
1 tablespoon granulated sugar
1 cup milk, scalded, cooled

1/2 teaspoon salt
2 cups all-purpose flour
Oil for deep-frying
Powdered sugar, sifted

In a small bowl, stir yeast into water; let stànd 3 to 4 minutes to soften. In a large bowl, beat eggs and granulated sugar until blended. Stir in milk, yeast mixture and salt. Using a whisk, beat in flour until mixture is smooth. Cover bowl with a dry towel; set in a warm place to rise until bubbly, 45 to 60 minutes. In a large skillet, pour oil for deep-frying 1-1/2 to 2 inches deep. Over medium-high heat, bring oil to 375F (190C). Pour 1 cup batter into a pastry bag fitted .with a 1/4-inch tip, a heavy plastic bag with a 1/4-inch opening cut in a corner or in a squeezable plastic bottle with a narrow tip. Squeeze batter through opening into hot oil, swirling in a circular design similar to a *bird's nest,* 3 to 4 inches in diameter. Fry 1 minute on each side or until golden brown. Use a slotted spoon to lift cooked crullers from hot oil. Drain on paper towels. Dust with powdered sugar. Serve hot. Makes 15 crullers.

Norwegian
❖ Independence Day Buffet ❖

On the 17th of May, up go the Norwegian flags. Choirs sing. Bands march in parades. Not only is *Sytende Mai* the anniversary of the Norwegian Constitution—adopted at Eidsvall in 1814—but the awakening of new life after long winter months.

The celebration is particularly merry in northern Norway where winters are long and cold. A famous celebration is held in the little village of Rjukan, situated in a narrow valley between mountains 6,000 feet high. Rjukan has no sun from late fall to the middle of March. The highlight of the festival is the arrival of the *Prince of the Sun,* who ascends his throne and issues the order of the day: "Let there be merriment until dawn!"

And merriment there is, as young and old dance in carnival costumes. Fireworks and bonfires are traditional and stem back to pagan customs of chasing away evil spirits.

Lefse and *Eggedosis* are typical of the foods served for Sytende Mai. Lefse is served at all special occasions in Norway. It belongs on a celebration menu whether it is for Sytende Mai, a wedding or an anniversary. Lefse is especially good with Fish Mousse. Nobody makes Fish Mousse like a Norwegian! Light in texture and wonderfully flavored, the creation is beautiful to look at when oven-poached in a pretty ring mold.

Although Eggedosis is a strange name, it is really a delightfully rich and thick eggnog-type dessert. Norwegians reserve it for special occasions and holidays. It is traditionally included on the Easter-dinner menu and is often served at Christmas.

As you plan a dinner party around this menu, choose between Fish Mousse with Shrimp Sauce and Jarlsberg Cod. The other offerings will complement either of these main dishes.

Norwegian Independence Day Buffet
Cheese Mousse (Oste Fromage), Crisp Crackers
Potato Flatbread (Lefse), page 31
Fish Mousse (Fiskepudding), Shrimp Sauce (Rekesaus)
Jarlsberg Cod (Jarlsberg Torsk)
Smörgås Salad Platter (Salatsauser med Rømme)
Trondheim Lemon-Raisin Soup (Trondhjem Suppe)
Cardamom Crackers (Goro)
Norwegian Egg Cream (Eggedosis)
Fruit-Juice Glögg (Saft Glögg), page 88
Mineral Water, Beer

Cheese Mousse

Oste Fromage—Norway

Serve this as an appetizer spread for crackers and flatbreads.

1 (1/4-oz.) envelope unflavored gelatin
1/2 cup cold water
2/3 cup half and half
3 egg yolks, slightly beaten

4 oz. Danish blue cheese, crumbled
3/4 cup whipping cream, whipped
Radishes, watercress and black olives for
  garnish

Lightly oil a 2- to 2-1/2-cup decorative mold; set aside. In a small bowl, sprinkle gelatin over cold water; set aside to soften. In a heavy, medium saucepan, combine half and half and egg yolks. Stir with a whisk over low heat until mixture cooks and thickens. Stir in softened gelatin and blue cheese; whisk until mixture is smooth. Refrigerate until texture resembles unbeaten egg whites, 30 to 45 minutes. Fold in whipped cream. Pour into prepared mold. Cover and refrigerate until set, 3 to 4 hours. Invert onto a round, medium platter; garnish with radishes, watercress and olives. Makes about 2 cups or about 12 servings.

Fish Mousse

Fiskepudding—Norway

This is the highlight of Norwegian cuisine—wonderfully light, airy and beautiful.

1-1/2 lbs. fresh or frozen pike, sole,
  haddock or cod fillets
2 teaspoons salt
1/4 teaspoon ground white pepper
Dash ground nutmeg
1-1/2 tablespoons cornstarch

1-1/3 cups milk
1-1/2 cups whipping cream
1 tablespoon butter
About 1/4 cup soft breadcrumbs
Chopped fresh parsley
Shrimp Sauce, page 62

Thaw frozen fish. Skin and bone fish, if necessary. Use paper towels to wipe fish dry. Cut fish crosswise into strips. Put fish strips through food grinder 3 times or until pureed. In large bowl of electric mixer, combine pureed fish, salt, pepper, nutmeg and cornstarch. Beat with electric mixer on high speed 10 minutes. Beat 20 minutes longer, gradually beating in milk and whipping cream. Or, fit food processor with steel blade; turn processor on. Drop fish fillets through feed tube; process until pureed. Add salt, pepper, nutmeg and cornstarch. While processing, gradually pour in milk and cream. Process in batches if processor bowl is small. Continue processing until mixture is light and fluffy. Preheat oven to 375F (190C). Butter a 10-cup ring mold or fancy tube mold and coat with breadcrumbs. Butter center of a 12-inch square of parchment paper, waxed paper or foil. Gently spoon whipped fish mixture into mold. Cover with buttered paper or foil, lightly pressing onto surface of fish mixture. Place mold in a 13" x 9" baking dish. Pour boiling water 1 inch deep into baking dish. Bake 45 minutes or until mixture pulls away from side of pan and a knife inserted in center comes out clean. Prepare Shrimp Sauce while mold bakes. Invert hot mousse onto a warmed serving dish. Sprinkle with chopped parsley. Serve immediately with hot Shrimp Sauce. Makes 8 servings.

Cheese Mousse; Smörgås Salad Platter, page 63; Mrs. Olson's Flour Lefse, page 124.

Jarlsberg Cod

Jarlsberg Torsk—Norway

Creamy Jarlsberg cheese and tomatoes make a delicious topping for baked cod.

1-1/2 lbs. fresh or frozen cod fillets
1 tablespoon butter
2 teaspoons salt
1 teaspoon ground white pepper

4 tomatoes, sliced
2 cups shredded Jarlsberg or
    baby Swiss cheese (8 oz.)
1/2 cup whipping cream

Thaw frozen fish. Remove skin and bones, if necessary. Use paper towels to wipe fish dry. Preheat oven to 375F (190C). Spread butter over bottom of a 13" x 9" baking dish. Arrange dry fish in dish. Sprinkle with salt and white pepper. Top with tomato slices, covering fish completely. Sprinkle with cheese and pour cream over top. Bake 25 minutes or until fish flakes when pierced with a fork. Makes 4 servings.

Trondheim Lemon-Raisin Soup

Trondhjem Suppe—Norway

This slightly sweet, faintly lemon soup makes a perfect luncheon, supper or dessert dish.

6 cups boiling water
1/2 cup short- or medium-grain rice,
    uncooked
1 cup light or dark raisins
3 tablespoons fresh lemon juice

2 tablespoons sugar
1/2 cup whipping cream
1/8 teaspoon salt
2 egg yolks, beaten

In a 3- or 4-quart saucepan, combine water, rice and raisins. Bring to a boil over high heat. Reduce heat to low; simmer 20 minutes or until rice is tender. In a small bowl, combine lemon juice, sugar, cream, salt and egg yolks. While slowing beating with a whisk, add lemon mixture to hot soup. Serve hot or cold. Makes 8 servings.

Shrimp Sauce

Rekesaus—Norway

This is excellent served with poached fish or Norwegian Fish Mousse, page 60.

1/4 cup butter
1/4 cup all-purpose flour
1/4 cup whipping cream
2 cups milk
1-1/2 teaspoons salt

1/4 teaspoon white pepper
2 tablespoons sherry, if desired
2 lbs. cooked, tiny shrimp
2 tablespoons dried dill weed or
    chopped fresh dill

Melt butter in a medium saucepan; stir in flour. Add cream and milk, whisking to keep mixture smooth. Cook and stir over medium heat until thickened and smooth. Stir in salt, pepper and sherry, if desired. Add shrimp; stirring occasionally, cook until shrimp are heated through. Stir in dill. Serve hot. Makes 4 cups.

Smörgås Salad Platter

Photo on page 61.

Salatsauser med Rømme—Norway

Guests make their own salads from this lovely presentation of fresh vegetables.

Cream Dressing, see below
2 heads Boston, butter or bib lettuce
1 large avocado, sliced,
    sprinkled with lemon juice
2 tomatoes, cut in thin wedges
2 cups sliced mushrooms

1 (16-oz.) can pickled beets,
    cut in julienne strips
1 cup sliced radishes
1/2 cup sliced green onions
1/2 lb. spinach, washed, shredded

Cream Dressing:
1 cup whipping cream
2 tablespoons chili sauce
1/2 teaspoon salt

1/4 teaspoon ground white pepper
Curry powder to taste

Prepare Cream Dressing; refrigerate until chilled. Arrange vegetables on a salad platter. Cover and refrigerate until ready to serve. To serve, have guests assemble their own salad, selecting from offerings on platter. Spoon dressing over individual salads. Makes 10 to 12 servings.

Cream Dressing:
In a small bowl, beat cream until stiff peaks form. Fold in remaining ingredients.

Norwegian Egg Cream

Eggedosis—Norway

Grownups like this thick, whipped, egg cream with a bit of brandy.

8 egg yolks
1/2 cup sugar

Brandy, if desired

In small bowl of electric mixer, beat egg yolks 10 minutes at high speed, adding sugar 1 tablespoon at a time. Spoon into small stemmed glasses or small individual dessert dishes; serve immediately. Add 1 tablespoon brandy to each glass or dessert dish before adding egg cream, if desired. Makes 8 servings.

Clarified Butter

Melt any amount of salted or unsalted butter in a heavy, medium saucepan over low heat. Butter will separate as it heats. Cook until milky portion at the bottom evaporates. Do not let mixture brown. Place a fine strainer or a sieve lined with several layers of cheesecloth over a glass jar. Pour remaining oily mixture through strainer or sieve. Cover jar; store in refrigerator up to 4 weeks. Or store in freezer up to 4 months.

Cardamom Crackers

Goro—Norway

Make these on a "goro" iron, page 7, then break the crackers into 3 servings.

3 eggs
1 cup sugar
1 cup whipping cream, whipped
1 cup butter, melted

1/4 teaspoon salt
1 teaspoon ground cardamom
6 cups all-purpose flour

Cut a paper pattern the same size as *goro iron;* set aside. In a large bowl, combine all ingredients in order given, mixing until thoroughly blended. Dough will be stiff. Divide dough into 4 equal pieces. On a lightly floured surface, roll out each piece to a rectangle 1/8 to 1/16 inch thick. Cut dough same size and shape as paper pattern. Place goro iron on stovetop over medium heat until a drop of water sizzles and bounces when dropped on iron. Brush inside of iron with shortening. Place 1 piece of cut-out dough on hot iron. Close iron and bake over medium heat 1 to 2 minutes on each side until golden brown. Remove crackers from iron. Cool on a rack; repeat with remaining dough. Separate into individual crackers. Makes about 36 crackers.

How to Make Cardamom Crackers

1/Cut a paper pattern the same size as *goro iron.* Trace pattern on dough.

2/Bake dough over medium heat until golden brown on both sides. Cool on a rack.

❖ Nameday Dinner ❖

In Sweden and Finland, it is traditional to celebrate your *nameday* rather than your *birthday*. This is a legacy of times past. Birthday celebrations were discouraged. But people were allowed to celebrate the day of the saint after which they were named. For instance, if your name is Beatrice, you will observe St. Beatrice's day on the second day of December.

Today, namedays are convenient when people do not want to give their ages. Children observe birthdays up to their teens, but most Scandinavian women celebrate their nameday. Men celebrate their nameday until they reach fifty.

When a man has his fiftieth birthday, a great celebration is planned. The more prominent the person in the community or country, the bigger the party. He invites all his friends, work associates and relatives to celebrate his marking of a half-century. Some men have a big reception in a hotel or public place. Many have an open house at home with a several-course meal. There is toasting with champagne and gifts. Because of the expense, some families plan and save for years for this special occasion.

The suggested menu is not lavish, but is festive. You may serve all of the courses, or choose only one dish and a dessert from this party-for-eight menu. To serve it Scandinavian-style, there must be toasting with champagne, or with the traditional schnapps and beer.

Schnapps is to be gulped in one swallow and is followed with beer as a chaser. Schnapps glasses hold about two tablespoons of liquid. After it is gulped, you are to hold the glass upside down on top of your head to show that it is empty. When I expressed hesitancy to gulp it, I was politely told it is all right for ladies to sip. What a relief!

Nameday Dinner

Herring Cocktail (Sillcocktail)
Swedish Limpa (Limpa), page 135
Swedish Mushroom Soup (Svampsoppa)
Crisp Cheese Sticks (Oststänger), page 57
Royal Pot Roast of Beef (Slottsstek)
Hasselback Potatoes (Hasselbackpotatis)
Steamed-Vegetable Platter (Grønsaksfat)
Mocha Torte (Mockatårta)
Red or White Wine, Coffee, Tea

Hasselback Potatoes

Hasselbackpotatis—Sweden

These attractive scored potatoes can be baked in a roasting pan with any roast.

6 to 8 baking potatoes
1/4 cup butter, melted

About 1 teaspoon salt
1/4 cup fine dry breadcrumbs

Butter a 13'' x 9'' baking dish; set aside. Preheat oven to 400F (205C). Peel potatoes; place in ice water to prevent browning. Dry 1 potato at a time with paper towels. Place dry potato in a ladle or deep spoon. Using a sharp knife, slice potato crosswise in 1/8-inch slices only to edge of ladle or spoon, not all the way through. Return scored potatoes to ice water. Drain on paper towels. Arrange, cut-side up, in prepared dish. Brush with half of butter; sprinkle with salt. Bake 30 minutes or until tender. Brush with remaining butter; sprinkle with crumbs. Bake 15 minutes longer or until browned. Makes 6 to 8 servings.

Swedish Mushroom Soup

Svampsoppa—Sweden

If chanterelle mushrooms are available in your area, they are excellent in this soup.

3 tablespoons butter
1 lb. fresh mushrooms, thinly sliced
1/2 teaspoon salt
1/4 teaspoon ground white pepper
1/3 cup all-purpose flour

About 2 qts. beef or chicken broth
1 cup whipping cream
1 teaspoon lemon juice
Salt and ground white pepper to taste
1/4 cup dry sherry

Melt butter in a 3- to 4-quart heavy saucepan over low heat. Add mushrooms; sauté over low heat until mushroom juices being to flow. Pour mushroom juice into a 2-cup measure; set aside. Stir 1/2 teaspoon salt, 1/4 teaspoon white pepper and flour into drained mushrooms. Add broth to mushroom juice to make 2 cups. Stir into mushroom mixture. Stir in 6 cups of remaining broth. Over high heat, cook and stir until soup is thickened, about 5 minutes. Stir in cream and lemon juice. Add salt and white pepper to taste. Stir in sherry. Serve hot. Makes 8 servings.

Herring Cocktail

Sillcocktail—Sweden

Serve this first course in stemmed glasses, punch cups or small dessert bowls.

1 (8-oz.) jar herring tidbits in wine sauce
4 medium potatoes, boiled, peeled
8 butter- or Boston-lettuce leaves
1/2 cup dairy sour cream
1/4 teaspoon salt

1/8 teaspoon ground white pepper
1 tablespoon minced green onion
1 teaspoon lemon juice
Dried dill weed or fresh dill sprigs or
**   chopped chives**

Drain herring. Slice potatoes. Place a lettuce leaf in each of 8 small dishes. Dividing evenly, arrange sliced potatoes and drained herring on lettuce. In a small bowl, combine sour cream, salt, pepper, green onion and lemon juice. Spoon a dollop of sour-cream mixture on top of each serving. Garnish with dill or chives. Makes 8 servings.

How to Make Hasselback Potatoes

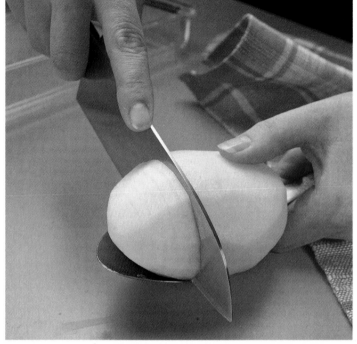

1/Place potato in a large spoon. Use a sharp knife to cut crosswise in 1/8-inch slices only to edge of spoon.

2/Brush with half of melted butter. Bake 30 minutes. Brush with remaining butter. Sprinkle with crumbs.

Royal Pot Roast of Beef

Slottsstek—Sweden

Flaming brandy adds flavor to the roast and to the drippings.

1 teaspoon salt
1 teaspoon ground allspice
1/2 teaspoon freshly ground black pepper
1 (4- to 4-1/2-lb.) boneless beef
   chuck roast
3 tablespoons butter
3 tablespoons brandy, if desired

1/3 cup beef broth
2 medium onions, sliced
3 anchovy fillets, minced
2 bay leaves
2 tablespoons white vinegar
2 tablespoons dark corn syrup

Combine salt, allspice and pepper. Rub over entire surface of beef. Melt butter in a 6-quart Dutch oven or heavy stewing pot. Add meat; brown on all sides. If used, pour brandy into a small sauce-pan. Warm over low heat; ignite. Pour over meat. Add broth, onions, anchovies, bay leaves, vinegar and corn syrup. Cover pot. Simmer over very low heat 2 hours or until tender. Place beef on a platter; keep warm. Pour drippings through a sieve into a large bowl. Return strained drippings to pot. Stir occasionally over medium-high heat, boiling until only 2 cups drippings remain. Spoon about 1/4 cup drippings over beef as a glaze. Pour remaining drippings into a serving bowl; serve with roast. Makes 8 servings.

Steamed-Vegetable Platter

Grønsaksfat—Scandinavian

The variety of vegetables makes a pretty platter.

1 (1-1/2- to 2-lb.) cauliflower head,
   trimmed
Boiling water
1-1/2 lbs. broccoli, trimmed
1/2 to 1 lb. zucchini squash, sliced

1 lb. carrots, peeled, cooked
1/4 cup butter, melted
1 teaspoon dried leaf tarragon or basil
Salt and pepper to taste

Place whole cauliflower in a deep, large saucepan; add 1 inch boiling water. Cover; cook over medium heat 5 minutes. Add broccoli; cook 5 minutes. Add zucchini; cook 5 minutes. Drain vegetables; arrange cooked cauliflower, broccoli, zucchini and carrots on a large platter. Drizzle with butter; sprinkle with tarragon or basil and salt and pepper to taste. Makes 8 servings.

Mocha Torte

Mockatårta—Sweden

This lovely meringue layer cake has a smooth, mild, coffee-flavored filling.

Meringue Layers, see below
1/3 cup ground coffee beans
1/2 cup water
1 cup half and half
3 egg yolks, slightly beaten

1-1/2 tablespoons cornstarch
1 cup unsalted butter, room temperature
1 cup powdered sugar
1 teaspoon vanilla extract
1/3 cup slivered almonds, toasted

Meringue Layers:
4 egg whites
1/2 teaspoon cream of tartar

1-1/4 cups sugar

Prepare Meringue Layers. In a small saucepan, bring coffee and water to a boil; let steep 5 minutes. Place a sieve over top of a double boiler. Line sieve with a coffee strainer. Pour coffee mixture into sieve. Discard coffee grounds. To coffee liquid, add half and half, egg yolks and cornstarch. Beating with electric mixer on high speed, cook over simmering water until mixture is thick and smooth. Cover pan; set aside. In small bowl of electric mixer, cream butter and sugar; add vanilla. Beat in coffee mixture, 1 tablespoon at a time, until smooth and fluffy. If mixture begins to curdle, place bowl over hot water and continue beating until smooth and fluffy. Cool to room temperature. Place a meringue layer on a round platter. Spread 1 cup filling over top. Place second meringue on top. Spread remaining filling over top. Sprinkle with almonds. Refrigerate at least 3 hours before serving. Makes 16 small servings.

Meringue Layers:
Grease and flour a large baking sheet. Draw 2 (9-inch) circles in flour on baking sheet. Preheat oven to 250F (120C). In a large bowl, beat egg whites until frothy. Add cream of tartar. Beat constantly while adding sugar, 1 tablespoon at a time. Beat until stiff and dry. Spread half of meringue in each circle on baking sheet, making flat and even. Bake 2 to 2-1/2 hours or until meringues are a creamy yellow color. Turn off oven. Leave meringues in closed oven to cool.

Steamed-Vegetable Platter; Swedish Limpa, page 135.

DINNERS & BUFFETS
❖ Danish Roast-Beef Buffet ❖

It is with great and calculated care that tiny Denmark produces food. The average Danish farm is only 25 acres, but is an excellent example of efficiency. Three-fourths of the total acreage of Denmark is devoted to agriculture. Of that, ten percent is used for hay, oats, rye, wheat and root crops. Almost all of the Danish farm income comes from animal products—butter, cheese, pork, beef, poultry and eggs. Danes produce more beef than all other Scandinavian countries.

As you drive through the Danish countryside, you see little *gaards,* or farms, nestled in the slightly rolling hills. A U-shaped cluster of thatch-roofed, whitewashed buildings forms the hub of the gaard. It is so neat and tidy that it is difficult to pick out the house from the barn. The buildings include the farmhouse, cow barn, pig stall and machine shed. The center of the U is a neat little courtyard.

Charming Danish *kroers* or country inns, sidewalk cafes and restaurants offer an elaborate and creative variety of cuisines. Danes love good food. Homecooked meals are plain and thrifty. They are always tasty and beautifully presented, even to family members around the cloth-covered kitchen table.

When guests are invited, the meal is planned as lavishly as for a king. The hostess takes great pains to set a beautiful table. With imagination and an artistic eye, she skillfully arranges flowers, candles and flags. Lovely porcelain figurines may set off her classic blue and white Royal Copenhagen china. The meal becomes an evening of entertainment around the table. Talk and laughter begin and end the meal, with jokes and stories interspersed.

Danish cuisine reflects a more continental flare than the rest of Scandinavia. It is characterized by careful attention to seasoning, detail and a feel for adventure.

For a festive occasion, serve schnapps as the Danes do, in tiny cordial glasses. Provide good Danish beer as a chaser. They also serve red wine, mineral water, milk, buttermilk and juices.

Danish Roast-Beef Dinner
Savory Tartlets (Tarteletter)
Danablu Tomatoes (Tomater med Danablu)
Danish Roast Beef (Oksesteg)
or
Spiced Danish Meatballs (Krydrede Frikadeller)
Danish Red Cabbage (Rødkål)
Caramelized Carrots (Glaserede Gulerødder)
Mocha Mousse (Mokkafromage)
Aquavit, Schnapps, Danish Beer, Milk, Coffee

Savory Tartlets   Photo on page 73.

Tarteletter—Denmark

For a pretty presentation, bake all three fillings in sandbakelser tins, page 8.

1-1/2 cups all-purpose flour
1/2 cup butter
1/4 teaspoon salt
1 egg, beaten

2 teaspoons lemon juice
1 to 2 tablespoons ice water
Choice of fillings, see below

Ham & Spinach Filling:
2 tablespoons butter
2 tablespoons all-purpose flour
1 cup half and half or milk

1 cup finely diced cooked ham
1 (10-oz.) pkg. frozen chopped spinach,
    cooked, squeezed dry

Crab & Shrimp Filling:
2 tablespoons butter
1 tablespoon all-purpose flour
1 (8-oz.) pkg. frozen snow crab, thawed
1 teaspoon anchovy paste

1/4 lb. or 1 (4-oz.) pkg. frozen tiny
    cocktail shrimp, thawed, drained
Paprika

Mushroom Filling:
2 tablespoons butter
1/4 lb. mushrooms, sliced
1 tablespoon all-purpose flour
1/2 teaspoon salt

1/4 teaspoon ground allspice
1 tablespoon dry sherry
Chopped fresh parsley

In a medium bowl or food processor fitted with steel blade, blend flour, butter and salt until mixture resembles coarse crumbs. In a small bowl, combine egg, lemon juice and 1 tablespoon ice water. Stir into flour mixture only until moistened. Add more ice water, if necessary. Gather dough into a ball. Wrap in plastic wrap; refrigerate 30 minutes. Divide dough into fourths. On a lightly floured board, roll out one-fourth of dough until 1/8 inch thick. Arrange 6 (1-1/2-inch) *sandbakelser* or *tartlet tins* close together near board. Wrap rolled-out dough around rolling pin. Without stretching dough, lift and gently unroll over tins. Gently lift and drape dough so it falls into tins. Roll rolling pin firmly over tins, cutting dough. Remove excess dough. Press dough evenly into each tin, from bottom to top, so dough reaches top of mold. Do not let dough extend above top of mold. Pierce bottoms of shells. Repeat with remaining dough. Refrigerate 30 minutes. Prepare filling or fillings; set aside. Preheat oven to 400F (205C). Bake chilled pastry shells 8 to 10 minutes until golden. Cool 10 minutes in tins; remove from tins. Spoon fillings into shells. Makes 24 tartlets.

Ham & Spinach Filling:
Melt butter in a small saucepan over medium heat. Stir in flour until blended. Gradually stir in half and half or milk. Stir until sauce is thickened. Stir in ham and spinach. Makes 3 cups.

Crab & Shrimp Filling:
Melt butter in a small saucepan over medium heat. Stir in flour; add crabmeat and liquid. Stir until thickened. Stir in anchovy paste and shrimp. Sprinkle with paprika. Makes 2-1/2 cups.

Mushroom Filling:
Melt butter in a medium skillet over high heat. Add mushrooms; sauté until browned, 4 to 5 minutes. Sprinkle flour, salt and allspice over sautéed mushrooms; cook and stir until juices are thickened. Stir in sherry. Sprinkle with chopped parsley. Makes about 2-1/2 cups.

Danish Roast Beef

Oksesteg—Denmark

Select a tender cut of beef for the best results, then roast in foil to keep it juicy.

1 (3-1/2- to 4-lb.) boneless
   beef-loin roast
1/4 cup butter, room temperature
4 garlic cloves, crushed

1 tablespoon coarsely cracked black
   peppercorns
1 teaspoon coarse or kosher salt

Preheat oven to 375F (190C). Cut a piece of heavy-duty foil large enough to wrap roast. Spread butter over center of foil. Rub roast with garlic; press pepper and salt onto surface of roast. Place meat on center of buttered foil. Fold foil using drugstore wrap. Or bring ends of foil together; fold ends together until against roast. Fold sides of foil to make an airtight package. Place on a rack in a roasting pan. Roast 45 minutes for rare or 1 hour for medium rare. Remove foil. Pour meat drippings into a small saucepan. Place roast on rack in roasting pan. Adjust oven temperature to 400F (205C). Roast 10 to 15 minutes or until meat is browned. While meat browns, place saucepan over medium-high heat. Boil drippings until reduced to a shiny glaze. Pour glaze over roast before serving. Let roast stand 20 minutes for easier slicing. Makes 8 servings.

Spiced Danish Meatballs

Krydrede Frikadeller—Denmark

Slightly flattened two-inch balls make the frikadeller authentic.

1 cup fine dry breadcrumbs
1 cup milk
2 small onions, minced
2 eggs
1-1/2 teaspoons salt
1/2 teaspoon ground nutmeg
1/2 teaspoon ground allspice

1/4 teaspoon ground cloves
1/4 cup all-purpose flour
2 lbs. extra-lean ground beef
2 tablespoons butter
2 tablespoons cornstarch
2 cups beef broth

In large bowl of electric mixer, blend breadcrumbs and milk. Let stand 10 minutes. Add onions, eggs, salt, nutmeg, allspice, cloves, flour and meat. Beat with electric mixer on high speed until mixture is light and fluffy, about 10 minutes. Using 1/3 cup mixture at a time, shape like eggs. Flatten balls slightly. Melt butter in a large, heavy skillet over medium heat. Add meatballs; brown on both sides. Place cooked meatballs on a warm platter. When all are browned, add cornstarch to skillet; stir until lightly browned. Slowly stir in broth. Stir with a whisk until gravy is thickened. Place meatballs in gravy; heat through. Makes 8 servings.

When shaping meatballs or cookie dough, use a small ice-cream scoop for even portions.

Danish Roast Beef; Savory Tartlets, page 71; Danish Red Cabbage, page 74.

Caramelized Carrots or Potatoes

Glaserede Gulerødder i Kartoffler—Denmark

These are a wonderful accompaniment to pork or beef.

1-1/2 lbs. carrots, 3 to 4 inches long, or	Water
1-1/2 lbs. small, firm potatoes	1/4 cup sugar
1/2 teaspoon salt	1/4 cup butter

Peel or scrape carrots; remove tips and stems. Peel potatoes. Place scraped carrots or peeled potatoes in a large saucepan. Add salt and water to cover. Bring to a boil over high heat. Reduce heat until water simmers. Simmer 20 minutes or until tender; drain. To serve, heat sugar in a large, heavy skillet, stirring constantly, until caramelized or lightly browned. Add butter; stir until melted. Add cooked carrots or potatoes. Shake pan, or stir until evenly glazed and heated through, about 10 minutes. Serve immediately. Makes 8 servings.

Danish Red Cabbage
Photo on page 73.

Rødkål—Denmark

Red cabbage is a favorite Danish side dish usually served with Christmas roast goose.

1 medium head red cabbage	1 teaspoon salt
(about 1-1/2 lbs.)	1/4 cup sugar
2 tablespoons butter	1/4 cup red-currant jelly, if desired
1/2 cup vinegar, lemon juice or	
pickled-beet juice	

Remove outer leaves and core from cabbage. Shred cabbage very fine. Melt butter in a large pot. Add cabbage, vinegar or juice, salt and sugar; stir to distribute. Cover and cook over low heat until cabbage is tender, about 20 minutes. Stir in jelly, if desired. Serve hot. Makes 8 servings.

Danablu Tomatoes

Tomater med Danablu—Denmark

Tomatoes stuffed with a combination of apples, celery and blue cheese—very tasty!

8 firm, medium tomatoes	1 celery stalk, minced
1 large Golden Delicious or	1/4 lb. Danish blue cheese, crumbled
Winesap apple, unpeeled, chopped	1/2 cup mayonnaise
8 pimiento-stuffed green olives, chopped	Chopped fresh parsley

Place a sieve over a small bowl; set aside. Cut a 1/4-inch slice off top of each tomato to make lids. Scoop center flesh and seeds from tomatoes into sieve. Press through sieve; set aside. Discard seeds. Invert tomato shells and lids on paper towels; let drain 10 minutes. In a medium bowl, combine apple, olives, celery and blue cheese. Spoon evenly into drained tomatoes. Stir 2 tablespoons sieved tomato into mayonnaise. Top each filled tomato with a dollop of mayonnaise mixture. Serve remaining mayonnaise mixture in a small bowl. Top each serving with reserved lids, placing slightly to 1 side. Garnish with chopped parsley. Makes 8 servings.

How to Make Caramelized Carrots

1/Stirring constantly, heat sugar until melted and lightly browned. Stir in butter until melted.

2/Shake pan or stir carrots until evenly glazed and heated through.

Mocha Mousse

Mokkafromage—Denmark

Wonderfully rich, but light.

1 (1/4-oz.) envelope unflavored gelatin	3 eggs
1/4 cup water	1/4 cup sugar
4 oz. semisweet chocolate	1 cup whipping cream
1 teaspoon instant coffee powder	Whipped cream, slightly sweetened

In a small metal bowl, soften gelatin in water. Place over a pan of hot water and stir until gelatin dissolves. Add chocolate and coffee powder. Continue stirring over hot water until chocolate melts. In a large bowl, beat eggs until light and pale. Beat in sugar until fluffy. Gradually beat in chocolate mixture. Whip 1 cup whipping cream until stiff; fold into chocolate mixture. Pour into a serving dish or individual serving dishes. Serve immediately or refrigerate until chilled. Decorate with a dollop of slightly sweetened whipped cream. Makes 8 servings.

❖ January Fish-Platter ❖

January begins with a holiday, resolutions, cold weather and poached-cod dinners. Cod is probably the most popular and most often eaten of the ocean fishes. It is fished in Scandinavia in all months that have an "r" in them. Danes and Norwegians say that cod is at its best in January. The flavor is mild and the texture is perfect when poached until the flesh lies in broad, chalk-white flakes. It is also at its lowest price in January. Cod is a part of the traditional Danish New Year's Eve meal. Danes serve it with melted butter and lemon, then wash it down with beer and iced schnapps.

Norway claims to have more than 200 varieties of fish and one way to cook them all—by poaching. But fish must be absolutely fresh to satisfy Norwegian cooks. Most people buy their fish from a fishmonger, who keeps the fish alive in large water tanks. Danes use the expression, "fresh as a fish," just as other people might say "fresh as a daisy."

When we visited the quaint cobblestone-street village of Stavanger, Norway, we selected a little restaurant with an unpretentious warehouse-like front by the fishmarket and pier. After much deliberation, we chose from among the dozens of fish on the menu. While the chef tended to the poaching liquid and the rest of the menu, his assistant ran out to the market to buy the fish we had chosen. It came from the kitchen steaming hot, wonderfully fresh and delicately flavored. We were also served a melted-butter sauce and a hot-mustard sauce. It was pure perfection!

For a pretty presentation and simple service of this dinner, surround the cod with boiled potatoes and cooked vegetables. The only additional accompaniment you'll need is bread and butter. Dessert is a delicate Danish version of crepes stuffed with a mild orange butter. To be fancy, you can flame them with orange-flavored liqueur, or simply sprinkle the crepes with powdered sugar and reheat them under the broiler.

January Fish-Platter
Poached-Cod Platter (Nytårstorsk)
Dilled Shellfish (Keitetyt Ravut)
Melted-Butter Sauce (Smørsauce)
Hot-Mustard Sauce (Sennepssauce)
Danish Pumpernickel (Rugbrød), page 135
Crepes with Orange Butter (Pandekager med Orangesmør)
Beer, Mineral Water, Milk, Coffee

Dilled Shellfish

Keitetyt Ravut—Finland

This dish is always served cold with hot melted butter and lemon juice.

1 qt. tightly packed fresh dill heads and
  stems
3 qts. water
1 tablespoon salt
1 tablespoon sugar

3 lbs. live crayfish, frozen rock or
  slipper lobster or shrimp in shells
Hot melted butter
Lemon wedges

In a large pot, combine dill, water, salt and sugar. Bring to a boil over medium heat; simmer 10 minutes. Add crayfish, lobster or shrimp. Bring to a boil again. Remove from heat; let stand 15 minutes. Pour off excess liquid, leaving only enough to cover seafood. Refrigerate until chilled, 45 to 60 minutes. Drain off liquid. Arrange chilled seafood on a platter. Serve with melted butter and lemon wedges. Squeeze lemon juice over seafood; dip seafood into butter. Makes 6 servings.

Melted-Butter Sauce

Smørsauce—Denmark

This sauce is excellent with any poached or baked fish.

1/2 cup butter
1/4 cup all-purpose flour
1/2 teaspoon paprika

1/2 teaspoon salt
2 cups cold water

Melt 1/4 cup butter in a medium saucepan over medium heat. Stir in flour to make a smooth paste. Stir in paprika and salt. Stir in water. Continue stirring until mixture comes to a boil; keep hot. Before serving, stir in remaining 1/4 cup butter; beat until butter melts. Makes 2-1/2 cups.

Hot-Mustard Sauce   Photo on page 79.

Sennepssauce—Denmark

Prepare this sauce at least 2 hours before serving to let the flavors blend.

3 tablespoons white vinegar
2 tablespoons grainy prepared German or
  Swedish mustard
1 tablespoon dry mustard
3/4 teaspoon salt

1/4 teaspoon ground white pepper
1/4 cup sugar
1/8 teaspoon ground cardamom
1/2 cup olive oil or vegetable oil

In a small bowl, use a whisk to beat vinegar, prepared and dry mustards, salt, white pepper, sugar and cardamom. Gradually whisk in oil until sauce is thick. Makes about 1 cup.

Poached-Cod Platter

Nytårstorsk—Denmark

Serve this mild-flavored dish with Melted-Butter Sauce or Hot-Mustard Sauce, page 77.

3 lbs. fresh or frozen cod fillets
2 teaspoons salt
1/4 cup white vinegar
2 qts. water
1/4 cup butter, melted

1 lemon, cut in wedges
18 small potatoes, peeled, cooked
12 small carrots, peeled, cooked
1 lb. broccoli, trimmed, cooked
1/4 cup chopped parsley

Thaw frozen fish. Place cod in ice water 2 hours before cooking, or 2 hours and 45 minutes before serving. Drain; sprinkle with salt. Let stand 15 minutes; rinse off salt. In a large shallow saucepan, combine vinegar and water. Bring to a boil over medium-high heat. Add fish; heat until liquid simmers. Cover pan; set aside. Let stand 20 minutes or until fish is firm but flakes when probed with a fork; drain. Arrange poached fillets on a hot platter. Pour melted butter over fish. Arrange lemon wedges, hot cooked potatoes, carrots and broccoli around fish; sprinkle parsley over vegetables. Makes 6 servings.

Crepes With Orange Butter

Pandekager med Orangesmør—Denmark

Tender crepes accented with orange flavor complete this dinner.

1 cup all-purpose flour
Pinch salt
2 eggs, slightly beaten
1 cup milk
1/3 cup butter, melted
Shortening

Citrus-Flavored Butter, see below
1/2 cup orange-flavored liqueur or
   orange juice
1/3 cup sugar
1/4 cup butter

Citrus-Flavored Butter:
1/2 cup butter, room temperature
1/4 cup sugar

Grated peel of 1 orange
Grated peel of 1 lemon

In a medium bowl, combine flour and salt. Stir in eggs, milk and 1/3 cup melted butter. Beat with a whisk until blended. Let stand 15 to 30 minutes. Heat a 6-inch crepe pan over medium-high heat. Grease pan with shortening. Pour about 1/4 cup crepe batter into pan. Quickly swirl to cover bottom of pan, then immediately pour excess batter back into bowl. Cook until crepe is golden on bottom. Turn and cook 15 seconds or until sizzling stops. Stack cooked crepes on a sheet of waxed paper. Repeat until all crepes are cooked, adding shortening as needed. Prepare Citrus-Flavored Butter. To serve, spread each crepe with about 2 teaspoons Citrus-Flavored Butter; fold crepes in half, then in half again. Pour orange liqueur or orange juice into a heatproof serving pan or platter. Stir in sugar and 1/4 cup butter. Place over medium heat until butter melts. Add folded crepes; keep warm. Makes about 15 crepes.

Citrus-Flavored Butter:
In a small bowl, cream butter and sugar; blend in grated peels.

Poached-Cod Platter; Hot-Mustard Sauce, page 77.

❖ Scandinavian Game Buffet ❖

Historically, Scandinavians have included game birds in their diet. An old Swedish cookbook gives a recipe for "breast of crows braised with onions." Today, game birds are scarce and are a specialty dish.

We had the rare privilege of dining on breast of ptarmigan at the Pohjanhovi Restaurant in Rovaniemi, northern Finland. We had to place our order at least two weeks early so the chef could have fresh ptarmigan on hand. It was worth the wait. The ptarmigan had a delicate *game* flavor and was served in a rich, creamy sauce.

The traditional accompaniment for game birds is lingonberries, plain or sugared. Preserved lingonberries make an authentic substitute.

Pheasant, pigeon, ptarmigan, partridge, grouse or woodcock are game birds that may be cooked in the same manner as the quail in the following recipe. Quail is available in many supermarkets and large, well-stocked gourmet food stores in most countries. Lacking all of these, Cornish game hens or breasts of broiler-fryer chickens may be substituted. Of course, Cornish game hens and chicken will not have the same robust flavor as wild birds.

In northern Finland, reindeer often appears on restaurant menus. You have the choice of *käristys*—a stew-like mixture, or *paisti*—reindeer that is thinly sliced and quickly pan-fried with bacon. Smoked reindeer is a specialty and is often a part of a smörgasbord menu. Deer, elk and reindeer are the principle game meats in Scandinavia.

Choose between Pan-Roasted Game Hens and Aquavit Hens for your main dish in this menu. The tomatoes and potatoes are simple and easy, but should be prepared just before serving. Prepare the soup and dessert ahead of time.

Scandinavian Game Buffet
Spinach Soup (Spenatsoppa)
Pan-Roasted Game Hens (Ungstekt Vaktel)
or
Aquavit Hens (Kokt Höns)
Panned Cherry Tomatoes (Grillade Tomater)
Creamy Fried Potatoes (Skånskpotatis)
Grape Pudding (Krem)
Milk or Buttermilk, Fruit Juices, Beer, Coffee

Spinach Soup

Spenatsoppa—Sweden

Scandinavians sometimes top this velvety soup with sour cream.

1 tablespoon butter
1 lb. spinach or 1 (10-oz.) pkg.
   frozen spinach, thawed
1/4 cup all-purpose flour
2 cups chicken broth

1 teaspoon salt
1/4 teaspoon ground white pepper
1/4 teaspoon ground allspice
2 cups milk
1/2 cup whipping cream

Melt butter in a medium saucepan over medium heat. Add spinach; stir until heated through. Stir in flour until moistened. Over high heat, slowly stir in chicken broth; cook and stir until thickened. Puree in a blender or food processor; pour puree into saucepan. Add salt, white pepper, allspice, milk and cream. Stir over medium heat only until soup comes to a boil. Serve immediately. Makes 4 to 6 servings.

Aquavit Hens

Kokt Höns—Sweden

Swedes also cook duck, partridge and grouse this way.

1/4 cup butter
2 (16-oz.) Cornish game hens, halved
1 cup dry white wine or chicken broth
1 teaspoon dried dill weed

1/2 teaspoon dried leaf thyme
1/2 to 1 teaspoon salt
2 tablespoons aquavit, brandy or gin,
   if desired

Melt butter in a large, heavy skillet over medium heat. Add game hens; brown on all sides. Pour wine or chicken broth over browned hens. Add dill, thyme, 1/2 teaspoon salt and aquavit, brandy or gin, if desired. Cover and simmer 20 to 30 minutes or until hens are tender. Place cooked hens on a plate; keep warm. Skim fat from drippings, then boil drippings until a thick glaze forms. Return hens to skillet; spoon glaze over hens. When hot, if desired, sprinkle with remaining 1/2 teaspoon salt. Arrange glazed hens on a medium platter. Spoon glaze from skillet over top. Serve immediately. Makes 4 servings.

Panned Cherry Tomatoes

Grillade Tomater—Sweden

Cherry tomatoes are a common garden vegetable in Scandinavia.

3 tablespoons butter
1 pint cherry tomatoes, stemmed, washed

1/2 teaspoon salt

Melt butter in a large skillet over high heat. Add tomatoes; shake skillet so tomatoes roll around as they heat. Sauté 2 to 3 minutes or until tomatoes are heated through. Sprinkle with salt; serve immediately. Makes a pretty garnish for steaks, hamburger and chicken. Makes 4 servings.

Pan-Roasted Game Hens

Ungstekt Vaktel—Sweden

Cover these tiny game birds so they don't overcook and become tough and dry.

4 quail, partridge or wild pheasants
3 tablespoons butter
1 tablespoon lemon juice
3 tablespoons aquavit or brandy, if desired
4 slices white bread, toasted, buttered

1 teaspoon Dijon-style or
   Swedish-style mustard
2 tablespoons red-currant jelly
1/4 cup firm butter, cut in 1/2-inch cubes
1 to 2 tablespoons water, if necessary

Rinse hens; pat dry with paper towels. Split lengthwise unless very small. Melt 3 tablespoons butter in a large, heavy skillet over medium heat. Add hens and lemon juice; brown slowly on all sides. Cover and cook 20 to 30 minutes or until hens are tender. Pour aquavit or brandy, if used, into a small metal measuring cup. Warm over low heat. Ignite and pour over cooked hens. Place 1 slice buttered toast on each of 4 dinner plates; top each with a cooked hen. Keep warm. Stirring vigorously with a whisk, boil pan drippings over high heat until reduced to a thick glaze. Whisk in mustard and jelly then butter cubes, until melted and blended. If sauce separates, whisk in 1 to 2 tablespoons water. Spoon evenly over hens. Serve immediately. Makes 4 servings.

Creamy Fried Potatoes

Skånskpotatis—Sweden

Diced potatoes cook quickly in butter and are delicious served in cream.

4 large potatoes, peeled
1 medium onion
1/4 cup butter
1 to 1-1/2 cups water

3/4 cup whipping cream
1 teaspoon salt
1/2 teaspoon freshly ground black pepper
1/4 cup chopped fresh parsley

Cut potatoes in 1/2-inch dice; place in a bowl of ice water to prevent browning. Cut onion in 1/2-inch dice. Melt butter in a large skillet over high heat; add diced potatoes and onion. Shaking pan frequently, sauté until potatoes are golden brown. Add 1 cup water; use a spoon to arrange potatoes and onion in an even layer. Cook, uncovered, over high heat until water evaporates, about 10 minutes. If potatoes are not tender, add remaining 1/2 cup water; boil until water evaporates. Pour cream evenly over cooked potatoes and onion; sprinkle with salt and pepper. Over medium heat, bring almost to a boil. Stirring gently, simmer 5 to 10 minutes or until cream is reduced in volume and thickened to a smooth sauce. Spoon mixture into a serving dish. Garnish with parsley. Serve hot. Makes 4 to 6 servings.

Use the cooking water from fresh vegetables as the liquid for baking yeast breads or add to homemade soup for flavor and nutrition.

How to Make Pan-Roasted Game Hens

1/Stirring vigorously with a whisk, boil pan drippings over high heat until reduced to a thick glaze.

2/Use a whisk to stir in mustard and jelly, then butter, until melted and blended.

Grape Pudding

Krem—Norway

This favorite of young and old is light, refreshing and simple to prepare.

1/2 cup quick-cooking tapioca
5 cups bottled grape juice
1/2 cup sugar

Pinch salt
Whipped cream, slightly sweetened

In a large saucepan, combine tapioca, grape juice, sugar and salt. Stir and let stand 15 minutes. Stirring constantly, bring to a boil over high heat. Reduce heat to low. Continue to stir and cook 15 minutes or until very thick. Cover and cool. Pour into a serving bowl or individual dessert dishes. Serve at room temperature or refrigerate until chilled. Serve with slightly sweetened whipped cream. Makes 6 servings.

❖ Midsummer's Day Buffet ❖

By Midsummer's Day, spring fever has come to a head and summer is ready to blossom. June 24th is the longest day of the year in Scandinavia. In a large part of Scandinavia, the sun doesn't set. It just skims the horizon.

Some scholars believe the Midsummer's festival is a continuation of the old pagan fire festival in honor of Balder, the sun god. Pious Christians tried in vain to put an end to this heathen festival. They later changed the name of the celebration to honor St. John the Baptist. Now, midsummer is known in Finland as *Juhannuspaivä,* in Sweden as *Johannes Dop,* in Denmark as *Sankt Hans* and in Norway as *Johsok* or Sankt Hans.

In most places today, Midsummer's Day is celebrated by dancing around a Maypole—a tall pole or mast bedecked with leaves and flowers that is ceremoniously raised. It is a time for dancing, feasting, picnics and parties.

Midsummer's season is a perfect time to travel in Scandinavia. But it is best to check with the national tourist office of each country for a listing of special celebrations.

An annual celebration is held in Helsinki, Finland, in the national folk-museum park, *Seurasaari.* Here, colorfully costumed dancers, with flowers and ribbons streaming from their hair, demonstrate native dances. The setting is among transplanted historic country buildings. Girls dressed in national costumes sit on old-fashioned swings decorated with flowers. The Maypole is decorated. There are bonfires, fiddlers and accordian players. Demonstrators make all kinds of old-fashioned foods for the public to sample. Festivities start on Midsummer's Eve and continue through Midsummer's Day. It's a time for open-air parties, if the weather is good.

To transplant a bit of festivity to your area of the world, sponsor a cooperative smörgåsbord using the menu on page 97. Or, use the following menu, which is not grandiose, but full of delicious food ideas. The dishes can be prepared in advance. Salmon is traditional on most Midsummer's Day tables, perhaps because sport fishermen have been lucky. Even Salmon-in-a-Crust can be prepared ahead.

Midsummer's Day Buffet
Appetizer Platter (Smörgåsplattar)
Butter, Variety of Breads
Salmon-in-a-Crust (Lohipiirakka)
Horseradish Mayonnaise (Pepparrotsmajonnäs)
Sliced Tomatoes and Cucumbers
Carrot-Apple Salad (Morot och Äpplesallad)
Strawberry-Cream Cake (Bløtekake)
Fruit-Juice Glögg (Saft Glögg), Milk, Coffee

Appetizer Platter

Smörgåsplattar—Scandinavia

Add to or subtract from this mini-smörgåsbord as you wish.

2 (1/2-cup) sticks butter, room temperature
1 (3-oz.) can sardines
1 head Boston or butter lettuce
1 large, white sweet onion, sliced
1 large apple, sliced
1 (8-inch) European-style cucumber or
   other cucumber, thinly sliced
1/4 lb. smoked herring, whitefish,
   salmon or trout
1/2 to 1 lb. Herrgardsost, spiced
   noekkelost, gjetost, Gorgonzola,
   Edam, Gouda or Swiss cheese, sliced

1 cup sliced radishes
1/2 lb. bacon, cooked crisp
1 (2-oz.) jar whitefish, lumpfish or
   salmon caviar
1 (8-oz.) jar herring fillets in wine sauce
Cardamom Crackers, page 64, or
   purchased crackers
Danish Pumpernickel, page 135,
   thinly sliced

Place butter on 2 butter trays or stir and spoon into a serving bowl. Place on serving table. On a large serving tray, arrange remaining appetizer items, leaving sardines, caviar and herring in containers. Arrange crisp breads and pumpernickel in a basket or on a tray. Let guests serve themselves. Makes about 12 servings.

Horseradish Mayonnaise

Pepparrotsmajonnäs—Sweden

This is excellent with any cold fish.

1/2 cup whipping cream
1 cup mayonnaise

3 tablespoons grated fresh horseradish

In a medium bowl, beat cream until soft peaks form. Fold in mayonnaise and horseradish until blended. Refrigerate 15 to 30 minutes for flavors to blend. Makes about 2 cups.

Carrot-Apple Salad

Morot och Äpplesallad—Sweden

In Sweden, this salad is usually served with fish.

2 medium, tart apples
4 large carrots, peeled, shredded

1 tablespoon fresh lemon juice
Crisp lettuce leaves

Wash apple; cut in quarters and remove cores. Do not peel; cut in fine dice. In a large bowl, combine diced apples, carrots and lemon juice. Refrigerate at least 20 minutes to chill. Arrange lettuce leaves on 8 individual salad plates or on a large platter. Spoon salad onto lettuce-lined plates or platter. Makes 8 servings.

Salmon-in-a-Crust

Lohipiirakka—Finland

Every Finnish hostess has her own version of this fish pie.

2 lbs. fresh or frozen salmon fillets
2 tablespoons butter
1 tablespoon lemon juice
1 teaspoon salt
2 tablespoons minced fresh parsley
1 tablespoon dried dill weed
Salt and pepper to taste
Cottage-Cheese Pastry, below

1-1/2 cups cooked rice
1/4 cup butter, melted
3 hard-cooked eggs, sliced
1 egg, thoroughly beaten
Melted butter
Lemon wedges for garnish
Horseradish Mayonnaise, page 85

Thaw frozen salmon. Rinse fillets; wipe dry with paper towels. Melt 2 tablespoons butter in a large skillet over high heat. Add salmon fillets; sauté 2-1/2 minutes on each side. Sprinkle with lemon juice and 1 teaspoon salt. Trim cooked salmon fillets so they resemble shape of a fish, 15 inches long and tapering from 5 inches to 3 inches width. Set aside. In a small bowl, combine salmon trimmings, parsley, dill and salt and pepper to taste. Refrigerate at least 20 minutes. Cover a large ungreased baking sheet with parchment paper. Or, grease baking sheet; set aside. Prepare pastry. On a lightly floured surface, roll out half of pastry to make an 18 " x 8" oval. Shape one end to resemble a fish tail, not less than 6 inches wide. Arrange pastry on prepared baking sheet. Cut pieces of dough scraps to represent fins; press in place. Spread parsley mixture over pastry to within 2 inches of edge; top with rice. Drizzle with 1/4 cup melted butter. Top with a layer of hard-cooked eggs. Cut salmon fillets in 4- or 5-inch pieces for easier handling. Top eggs with cooked salmon fillets. Roll remaining half of dough to a 20" x 10" oval. Moisten edges on bottom crust with water. Arrange top crust over salmon layer. Press top and bottom crusts together, pressing with sides of your hands to seal. Trim, following lines of bottom crust, shaping fins and tail. Brush surface with beaten egg. Preheat oven to 375F (190C). Cut a hole where eye of fish should be. Insert a small ball of dough to keep hole open. With tips of scissor blades, cut top crust to simulate fish scales. These also serve as air vents during baking. Bake 35 minutes or until crust is lightly browned but still pale. To serve, cut in crosswise slices. Serve with melted butter, lemon wedges and Horseradish Mayonnaise. Makes 8 servings.

Cottage-Cheese Pastry

Rahkakuori—Finland

Use this lovely, flaky pastry for sweet or savory pies.

1 cup cold, firm butter
2 cups all-purpose flour

1 cup small-curd cottage cheese
1 to 2 tablespoons ice water, if needed

In a large bowl, cut butter into flour until mixture is crumbly and pieces are about the size of peas. Stir in cottage cheese until mixture forms a crumbly dough. Knead lightly to shape into a ball, adding ice water a few drops at a time, if necessary. Chill 30 minutes before rolling out. Makes enough pastry for a 9-inch double-crust pie.

How to Make Salmon-in-a-Crust

1/Spread parsley mixture over bottom pastry, to within 2 inches of edge. Top with rice.

2/Top rice with a layer of egg slices. Arrange trimmed sautéed salmon over egg slices.

3/Press top and bottom crusts together, pressing with sides of your hands to seal. Trim even with bottom crust.

4/Insert a small ball of dough for eye. With tips of scissor blades, clip top crust to resemble fish scales.

Strawberry-Cream Cake

Bløtekake—Norway

This is the most popular of the decorated cakes in Scandinavia.

1/3 cup all-purpose flour	Custard Filling, see below
1/4 cup cornstarch	1 pint fresh strawberries
1 teaspoon baking powder	1-1/2 cups whipping cream
4 eggs, separated	2 tablespoons powdered sugar
3/4 cup granulated sugar	1 teaspoon vanilla extract

Custard Filling:

2 egg yolks, slightly beaten	1 cup half and half
1-1/2 tablespoons butter	2 tablespoons sugar
1 tablespoon cornstarch	2 teaspoons vanilla extract

Butter a 9- or 10-inch springform pan; dust with flour; set aside. Preheat oven to 350F (175C). In a small bowl, combine flour, cornstarch and baking powder. In a large bowl, beat egg whites until fluffy. Gradually beat in granulated sugar until stiff peaks form; set aside. In a small bowl, beat egg yolks until pale. Fold beaten egg yolks, then flour mixture into beaten egg whites. Pour batter into prepared pan. Bake 30 minutes or until top of cake feels dry. Center of cake will be slightly indented. Let stand 5 minutes. Remove side of pan. Loosen cake from bottom of pan; cool cake on a rack. Prepare Custard Filling. Reserve 5 strawberries for top of cake. Slice remaining strawberries lengthwise; set aside. In a medium bowl, beat cream until stiff peaks form. Beat in powdered sugar and vanilla. When cake is cooled, cut horizontally into 3 thin layers. Place bottom layer on a cake platter; spread with half of Custard Filling and half of sliced strawberries. Place second cake layer on top. Spoon remaining Custard Filling and sliced strawberries over top. Place remaining cake layer on top. Spoon whipped-cream mixture over top of cake; decorate with reserved strawberries. Serve immediately or refrigerate until ready to serve. Makes 16 servings.

Custard Filling:

In a small saucepan, blend egg yolks, butter, cornstarch, half and half and sugar. Stirring constantly, cook over medium heat until smooth and thickened. Cover pan and set aside to cool. Stir vanilla into cooled custard.

Fruit-Juice Glögg

Saft Glögg—Sweden

This family-style glögg is popular in all of Scandinavia during Advent.

1 medium orange	1 (3-inch) cinnamon stick
1 qt. apple cider	8 whole cloves
2 cups white grape juice or currant juice	2/3 cup raisins
1/4 cup sugar	2/3 cup slivered blanched almonds

Using a vegetable peeler, cut colored portion from orange in a single spiral. Reserve orange for another purpose. In a large pot, combine orange peel and remaining ingredients. Let stand 4 hours. Bring to a boil over medium heat. Reduce heat to low; simmer 30 minutes. Serve hot or cold in punch cups, including some raisins and almonds in each serving. Makes 12 servings.

❖ Karelian Country-Style Dinner ❖

The food of Finland has more diversity than any other Scandinavian country. This is because Finland is a buffer zone between East and West. She shares a western border with Sweden and Norway and an eastern border with Russia.

Foods of western Finland reflect strong similarities with the rest of Scandinavia. In the east, the folk arts, handicrafts, poetry, music and food of Karelia have woven a special richness into Finnish life. The Finnish national epic, the *Kalevala,* and the Finnish national instrument, the *Kantele,* come from Karelia.

After the eastern part of Karelia was lost to Russia in 1939 and 1940, many of the people moved west and were welcomed into the homes of other Finns. Property was divided. Finns shared their wealth to help relocate and resettle the Karelians. People donated jewelry, money or whatever they had. A great aunt of ours, admiring my wedding rings, glanced at her left hand and remarked, "Yes, I had rings once, but I donated them to the Karelian cause."

Karelian cooking depends on the abundant use of the oven. This was a main point of friction between the "two women of the house." In western Finland, in the Spring and Fall, it was the custom to bake round, flat, rye bread with a hole in the center. The loaves were strung on poles and hung in the *aitta,* or grainery, to dry. This preserved them for the coming season. Karelians, on the other hand, baked their fat, round, sour-rye loaves every day. Karelians complained that the Finnish sour-rye bread was so tough it broke their teeth. The western Finns complained that the Karelians baked so much it cracked their ovens!

Because the oven was always hot, Karelians made *piirakka,* or meat pies. The most popular piirakka is a rice filling baked in a rye crust. Today Karelian piirakka are available in almost every supermarket, bakery, delicatessen and coffeeshop in Finland. Finns use them as popular lunchbox sandwiches. Restaurants serve piirakka as a base for *smørrebrød* sandwiches.

Karelian Country-Style Dinner
Karelian Ragout (Karjalan Paisti)
Baked Wild Rice (Minnesota Villiriisi)
Leaf-Lettuce Salad (Lehtisalaatti)
Karelian Pies (Karjalan Piirakka)
Egg Butter (Munavoi). Fruit Pudding (Marja Kiisseli)
Beer, Mineral Water, Milk, Buttermilk, Coffee

Karelian Pies

Karjalan Piirakka — Finland

These oval-shape pies in a rye crust reveal the rice filling through the top.

1 cup medium-grain rice, uncooked
1 cup water
About 3 cups milk
2 tablespoons butter
2 to 3 teaspoons salt

1/2 cup butter
1/2 cup milk
Rye Crust, see below
Egg Butter, page 92

Rye Crust:
1 cup water
2 tablespoons butter, melted
1 teaspoon salt

1-1/2 cups all-purpose flour
1-1/2 cups rye flour

In a medium saucepan, bring rice and water to a boil over high heat. Stir in 3 cups milk. Reduce heat to low; cover and cook until rice is tender, 20 to 25 minutes. Add 2 tablespoons butter and salt to taste. Beat with a wooden spoon until mixture is creamy. Add more milk, if necessary, until consistency is similar to cooked oatmeal. Set aside to cool. Grease 3 or 4 baking sheets or cover with parchment paper; set aside. Prepare a glaze by melting 1/2 cup butter in a small saucepan over low heat; stir in 1/2 cup milk. Stirring occasionally, heat until milk is hot; set aside and keep warm. Prepare Rye Crust. Spread 1/4 cup cooked rice filling on each dough circle to within 1 inch of edge. Fold uncovered edge of dough over filling, making a boat-shape oval, narrower and sharply pointed on two opposite ends. Leaving center open, crimp crust edge in even *pleats* as it is brought up over filling. Place pies, 2 to 3 inches apart, on prepared baking sheets. Preheat oven to 450F (230C). Brush pies with warm butter-and-milk glaze. Bake glazed pies 15 minutes. Brush with glaze after 7 minutes and again after removing from oven. Serve hot or cold with Egg Butter. Makes 16 pies.

Rye Crust:
In a large bowl, combine water, butter, salt and all-purpose flour; beat until smooth. Stir in rye flour to make a stiff dough similar to a yeast dough. Turn out onto board dusted with rye flour. Knead until smooth, about 5 minutes. Divide into 4 equal pieces. Cut each piece into fourths. Shape each piece into a ball. On lightly floured board, roll out each ball of dough to a 6-inch circle.

Baked Wild Rice

Minnesota Villiriisi — Finnish Americans

Bake this simple wild-rice dish in the oven with Karelian Ragout, page 92.

1 cup wild rice, uncooked
4 cups beef or chicken broth
1 teaspoon salt

1/2 teaspoon pepper
1 tablespoon butter

Preheat oven to 250F (120C). Wash wild rice in 3 changes of hot tap water. In a heavy 2-quart casserole dish, combine washed rice, broth, salt, pepper and butter. Cover and bake 3 hours. Fluff rice with a fork. Makes 8 servings.

How to Make Karelian Pies

1/Spoon rice mixture onto dough circle. Fold edges to form an oval.

2/Starting from center, crimp or pleat dough, leaving center open.

Leaf-Lettuce Salad

Lehtisalaatti—Finland

The simple lemon-cream dressing is especially good with fresh garden lettuce.

**2 qts. garden leaf lettuce or
   other salad greens, washed, dried**
1/4 cup fresh lemon juice
1 tablespoon sugar

1/2 teaspoon salt
Dash freshly ground black pepper
1/4 cup whipping cream

Tear lettuce greens in 1- to 2-inch pieces. Place in a salad bowl; refrigerate. To serve, combine lemon juice, sugar, salt and pepper in a small bowl. Beat with a whisk while slowly adding cream. Continue beating until blended and creamy. Drizzle dressing over lettuce; toss to distribute. Serve immediately. Makes 6 to 8 servings.

Karelian Ragout

Karjalan Paisti—Finland

In olden days, this was made from trimmings after the Fall butchering.

1 lb. lean stewing beef
1 lb. lean, boneless stewing lamb
1 lb. lean pork shoulder
1 medium onion, sliced
1 tablespoon salt

6 whole allspice
1 bay leaf, crumbled
1 (16-oz.) can whole small onions, drained
8 oz. fresh, whole, small mushrooms
Boiled whole potatoes or cooked wild rice

Trim fat from meat before weighing. Cut meat into 1-inch cubes. Preheat oven to 250F (120C). Separate sliced onion into rings. Layer meat and onion rings in a heavy 3-quart oven-to-table casserole dish, sprinkling each layer with salt. Top with allspice and bay leaf. Cover with a tight-fitting lid. Bake 3 hours; stir. Bake 3 hours longer or until meat is tender. Spoon canned onions and fresh mushrooms over meat mixture. Bake 15 minutes, uncovered. Spoon some of broth that has formed over potatoes or wild rice. Makes 8 servings.

Egg Butter

Munavoi—Finland

Use this spread on Karelian Pies, page 90, rye bread, sandwiches or toast.

1 cup butter, room temperature
1/4 teaspoon salt

1/8 teaspoon ground ginger
4 hard-cooked eggs, finely chopped

In a medium bowl, beat butter, salt and ginger until light and fluffy. Stir in eggs. Serve immediately or store in refrigerator. Serve at room temperature. Makes 2 cups.

Fruit Pudding

Marja Kiisseli—Finland

This dessert can be prepared in advance, and is good either hot or cold.

1 qt. water
3 cups fresh or frozen blueberries,
   raspberries, boysenberries,
   strawberries or blackberries

1/2 cup sugar
3 tablespoons cornstarch
Whipping cream

In a large saucepan, combine water and berries. Bring to a boil over medium heat, stirring to break up frozen fruit. In a small bowl, combine sugar and cornstarch. Slowly add to boiling fruit mixture while whisking vigorously. Stir and cook until thickened, about 15 minutes. If under-cooked, mixture may break down and become thin after cooling. Serve hot or cold. To serve, pour cream over individual servings. Makes 8 servings.

❖ Dinner in Finnish Lake Country ❖

One of the most scenic areas of Finland is found northeast of Helsinki, in the Saimaa Lake District. Travelers take a short train ride from Helsinki to the village of Lapeenranta. Here they board a comfortable Finnish steamer. It travels along a scenic northern route to Kuopio, a village situated in Karelia District. The trip takes you along pine-rimmed lakes very near the border of Russia.

In Kuopio, you can visit a colorful open market and purchase one of the world's most unique foods, a fish pie or *kalakukko*. Kalakukko is made fresh every day by homebakers and sold in the market, still warm from the oven. Exotic in its unusual flavor, kalakukko is simple to make with tiny, bony, fresh-water fish called *muikku,* a relative of herring. Baked long and slow, the bones soften so they melt in your mouth.

Kalakukko look like plump, round, loaves of rye bread. The thick rye crust acts almost as a casserole dish enclosing the filling. Finns make other *kukko* versions filled with beef chunks and potatoes or pork and turnips. The fish filling is the local favorite for picnics, lunches or snacks.

In our recipe, Kalakukko, or Fish Pâté, is made with pike or perch because of their availability. To serve this pâté, slice it like you slice a loaf of bread, or cut a slice off the top of the loaf and scoop out the savory filling. Break off pieces of the delicious rye crust to eat with the filling.

Dinner in Finnish Lake Country
Iron-Range Fish Stew (Kalamojakka)
Fish Pâté (Kalakukko)
Melted Butter & Lemon Wedges
Finnish Cucumber Salad (Kurkkusalaatti)
Strawberries & Cream or
Finnish Air Pudding (Ilmapuuro), page 119
Beer, Milk, Buttermilk, Coffee, Tea

Fish Pâté

Kalakukko—Finland

This bacon-flavored fish pie has the best flavor when it is served warm.

1-1/2 lbs. fresh or frozen, small pike, perch or trout	1/2 cup butter
Rye Crust, see below	1/2 cup water
1 teaspoon salt	Melted butter
1/2 lb. sliced bacon	Lemon wedges

Rye Crust:

4 cups stirred rye flour	2 cups warm water
1/2 to 1 cup all-purpose flour	2 tablespoons butter, melted
2 teaspoons salt	

Thaw frozen fish. Clean fish, removing entrails, head, tail and scales. It is not necessary to remove skin and bones. Prepare Rye Crust. Stack half of fish onto center of dough, leaving 4 inches on all sides uncovered. Sprinkle with 1/2 teaspoon salt. Top with bacon. Add remaining fish and salt. Fold sides of dough to center, over filling. Moisten edges slightly with water; pinch edges to seal. Preheat oven to 300F (150C). To prepare glaze, heat butter and water in a small saucepan over medium heat until butter melts. Grease a large baking sheet with raised sides. Place filled crust on center of baking sheet. Brush surface of pie with butter-and-water glaze. Make a 1-1/2-inch slash in top of crust. Bake 1-1/2 hours, brushing occasionally with glaze. Cut a piece of foil large enough to enclose pie. Place baked pie on foil; wrap airtight. Return wrapped pie to baking sheet; bake 3 hours longer. Turn off oven; leave pie in oven 2 hours longer or until oven has cooled. This will soften crust. To serve, slice crosswise, or cut a 3-inch oval out of top of crust. Scoop out filling. Serve hot, warm or cold. Spoon melted butter, then squeeze lemon juice over filling. Break off pieces of crust to serve with filling. Makes 4 dinner servings or 8 snack or appetizer servings.

Rye Crust:
In a large bowl, combine rye flour, 1/4 cup all-purpose flour and salt. Stir in water, then butter. Add enough all-purpose flour to make a stiff dough. Turn out onto a board lightly sprinkled with rye flour. Knead dough until smooth. Dough will feel similar to clay. Roll out dough to a 14-inch square, about 1/2 inch thick.

Finnish Cucumber Salad

Photo on pages 110-111.

Kurkkusalaatti—Finland

Thin slicing lets the marinade penetrate the cucumbers, making them crisp and tangy.

1 (10- to 12-inch) European-style cucumbers or 2 (6-inch) cucumbers	1/2 cup sugar
2 tablespoons dried dill weed	1/4 cup water
1/2 cup white vinegar	1 teaspoon salt

Cut cucumber in paper-thin slices. In a medium bowl, layer sliced cucumbers, sprinkling dill between layers. In a 2-cup measure, combine vinegar, sugar, water and salt. Pour over cucumber mixture. Refrigerate 4 to 5 hours. Makes 4 to 6 servings.

How to Make Fish Pâté

1/Fold dough over fish and bacon filling. Pinch to seal.

2/To serve, cut top from rye crust. Spoon out filling.

Iron-Range Fish Stew

Kalamojakka—Finnish Americans

The term "mojakka" means fish stew to American Finns—no one knows its origin.

3 lbs. fresh or frozen freshwater trout,
   walleye or whitefish fillets
6 large potatoes, peeled, cut in large cubes
1 large onion, diced
2 teaspoons salt
5 whole allspice

6 cups water
2 cups whipping cream or
   1 (13-oz.) can evaporated milk
2 tablespoons butter
1/4 teaspoon dried dill weed, if desired

Thaw frozen fish. Remove skin and bones, if necessary; set aside. In a large pot or soup kettle, combine potatoes, onion, salt, allspice and water. Cover and bring to a boil over medium heat. Reduce heat to low; simmer until potatoes are tender, 15 to 20 minutes. Cut fish in 2-inch pieces. Use a slotted spoon to add fish pieces to stew. Cover and simmer 15 minutes longer or until fish flakes easily. Do not boil. Fish will remain in pieces. Stir in whipping cream or evaporated milk, butter and dill, if desired. Serve hot. Makes 6 servings.

SMÖRGÅSBORDS

❖ Cooperative Smörgåsbord ❖

Smörgåsbord is not limited to Swedish celebrations. In Finland, it is called *voileipäpöytä*. Both words translate to *bread-and-butter table*. In Norway and Denmark it is called *koldtbord,* which means *cold table.* They all mean that the food served will be delicious with, or on, bread and butter.

Originally, a smörgåsbord was a community effort. According to legend, the horse and buggy ride to church on Sunday was a long one. Church services were not short, and people became very hungry. Families began bringing food to share— each woman bringing her specialty. Thus the smörgåsbord was born.

The smörgåsbord in modern Scandinavia follows the same menu pattern established years ago. Breads and butter are placed at the head of the table. They are followed by a selection of pickled and preserved herring, cold fish and meats, salads and cooked potatoes. Plain boiled potatoes are a part of every course but dessert. Next, the hot foods are served. Cheese, cold puddings and desserts come last.

There is a definite pattern to serving oneself at a smörgåsbord. Food is never heaped on a plate. The idea is to sample the foods a few at a time, making several trips to the table. This keeps the various flavors of foods separate and distinct.

The first course of the meal is always buttered bread and fish. When you return to the table for the next course, take a clean plate. This time, sample the cold smoked- and salted-fish combinations and cold meats. For the third course, take another clean plate and sample the hot foods. Next, taking another clean plate, sample the salads, cheese and hot and cold vegetable dishes. As a climax to the meal, take another clean plate and sample the desserts or the cheese and fruits. Coffee is served after dessert.

Serve your smörgåsbord on a round, square or oblong table large enough to hold all of the food without crowding. If the wood grain is pretty, the table may be left bare. Depending on the mood you want to convey, leave the table bare or cover it with a rough woven or a fine linen cloth. Place the food so the normal flow of traffic will take your guests from the first course to the last. By placing the plates, silverware, bread and cold fish dishes together, your guests will know where to start.

Scandinavians use natural table decorations. You will never see artificial flowers on a table in Scandinavia. In the Spring, the table may be decorated with sprouted branches of bushes or trees, or with a basket of pretty Easter eggs nestled in fresh foliage. In the Summer, they often use a small bucket of fresh wild flowers. At one home, a lovely glass bowl was filled with water and colorful rocks from the seashore. At another, for a Christmas celebration, a small pine tree was set in a tall candle holder and was decorated with candles. Candles are often used on the table. In Scandinavia, you can purchase candles in every color of the spectrum.

In Scandinavia, you seldom see a full smörgåsbord in a home. However, you may see an abbreviated version or *smörgåsplatter,* which makes a fine first course to a meal. To prepare all the dishes for a full smörgåsbord by yourself is a monumental task. It is better to follow the traditional pattern and invite others to a cooperative smörgåsbord. If this is not possible, have part or all of the meal catered by a hotel, restaurant or gourmet shop.

The menu that follows contains more dishes than could possibly be used at a single smörgåsbord. Select and prepare two or more items from each of the courses, with particular attention to variety of ingredients, color and flavor. *Skol!* or as the Finns say, *Kippis!*

Cooperative Smörgåsbord

First Course:
Glass-Master's Herring (Glasmästarsill)
Mustard Herring (Senapsill), page 50

Cold-Food Course:
Swedish Beef Tongue (Oxtunga)
Pressed Pork Roll (Käärysyltty), page 52
Danish Cucumber Salad (Agurkesalat)
Danish Curry Salad (Karrysalat)
Pineapple-Beet Salad (Ananas Punajuurisalaatti)

Hot-Food Course:
Fish Frikadeller (Fiskefrikadeller)
Jansson's Temptation (Janssons Frestelse)
Karelian Ragout (Karjalan Paisti), page 92
Rutabaga-Potato Casserole (Perunalanttulaatikko), page 115

Flatbreads, Swedish Limpa (Limpa), page 135

Bond Ost, Gammelost, Jarlsberg Cheeses
Smoked Farmer's Cheese (Rygeost)

Dessert Course:
Cranberry-Rye Pudding (Ruismarjapuuro)
Chocolate-Dipped Orange Sticks (Orangesmåkager), page 154

Red or White Wine, Coffee, Tea

Jansson's Temptation

Janssons Frestelse—Sweden

Serve this irresistible anchovy-and-potato casserole as a side dish or a midnight snack.

3 tablespoons butter
2 large onions, sliced
4 medium potatoes, peeled,
   cut in julienne strips

1 (3-oz.) can Swedish anchovy fillets
1 cup half and half

Butter a shallow 2-quart baking dish; set aside. Preheat oven to 400F (205C). Melt 1 tablespoon butter in a large skillet. Add onions; stirring occasionally, sauté 2 minutes or until soft but not browned. In prepared baking dish, alternately layer potatoes, sautéed onions and anchovies, beginning and ending with potatoes. Sprinkle 1 tablespoon brine from anchovies over top. Dot with remaining 2 tablespoons butter. Pour 1/2 cup half and half over top. Cover and bake 25 minutes. Remove cover; add remaining half and half. Bake 25 minutes longer. Serve hot or at room temperature. Makes 6 servings.

Glass-Master's Herring

Glasmästarsill — Swedish

The name comes from the procedure of layering herring and spices in a glass jar.

1 (16-oz.) jar herring fillets in wine sauce
1 teaspoon whole allspice, crushed
1 tablespoon pickling spices
1-1/2 tablespoons shredded fresh gingerroot
1/2 teaspoon mustard seeds
1/4 cup diced fresh horseradish
2 red onions, thinly sliced
1 small carrot, peeled, thinly sliced
1/2 cup sugar
3/4 cup white-wine vinegar

Drain herring and discard juices. In a small bowl, combine allspice, pickling spices, gingerroot, mustard seeds and horseradish. In a deep glass bowl or jar, layer half of the sliced onion and half of the carrot. Add all of drained herring. Sprinkle spice mixture over herring. Top with remaining onions and carrot. In a small bowl, combine sugar and vinegar. Pour over herring mixture. Cover and marinate in refrigerator 3 days. Serve from marinade bowl or jar. Makes about 16 herring pieces.

Variation

To increase servings, double amount of herring without doubling remaining ingredients.

Danish Curry Salad

Karrysalat — Denmark

Curry is often used in Danish and Norwegian cuisine.

Curry Dressing, see below
2 hard-cooked eggs, diced
1 (16-oz.) jar herring in wine sauce,
   drained, chopped
1 cup chopped cooked ham
1/2 cup diced cucumber
2 cups cold cooked rice
Crisp lettuce leaves
Fresh fennel for garnish, if desired

Curry Dressing:
1/4 cup whipping cream
1/2 cup mayonnaise or salad dressing
1-1/2 teaspoons curry powder
1/8 teaspoon salt
1/8 teaspoon ground white pepper
1 teaspoon white- or red-wine vinegar

Prepare Curry Dressing. In a large bowl, toss together eggs, herring, ham, cucumber and rice. Fold in dressing. Line salad bowl or platter with lettuce leaves. Spoon salad onto lettuce. Garnish with fennel, if desired. Makes 6 servings.

Curry Dressing:

In a medium bowl, whip cream until soft peaks form. Fold in remaining ingredients.

Swedish Beef Tongue

Oxtunga—Sweden

Serve this cold and thinly sliced, with mustard or a mustard sauce.

1 (3-lb.) beef tongue
1 onion, quartered
2 carrots, sliced

2 tablespoons mixed pickling spices
Water to cover

Scrub tongue under running water. Place tongue in a deep kettle; add onion, carrots, pickling spices and water to cover. Bring to a boil, then simmer 3- to 3-1/2 hours over low heat until tongue is tender when pierced with a fork. Cool in broth. Peel skin from tongue; cut away small bones and fatty portions. Refrigerate until ready to use. Strain broth; discard vegetables and spices. Reserve broth for sauces or soup. To serve tongue, slice thinly and arrange on a platter. Makes 20 to 24 appetizer servings.

Danish Cucumber Salad

Agurkesalat—Denmark

The marinade gives these crisp, paper-thin cucumber slices a sweet-sour flavor.

1 (16-inch) European-style cucumber or
  2 (8-inch) cucumbers
1 cup water
1 cup white vinegar

1/4 teaspoon ground white pepper
1/4 teaspoon salt
1 cup sugar

Cut cucumbers in paper-thin slices, making about 4 cups slices. In a large bowl, combine remaining ingredients; stir until sugar dissolves. Stir in cucumbers. Refrigerate 4 to 6 hours. Drain. Serve marinated cucumbers in a pretty glass bowl. Makes 6 to 8 servings.

Pineapple-Beet Salad

Ananas Punajuurisalaatti—Finland

Fast and easy to prepare.

1 (20-oz.) can pineapple chunks, drained
1 (16-oz.) can pickled beets, drained,
  cut in julienne strips
2 tablespoons white-wine vinegar
1/4 cup vegetable oil

3 tablespoons sugar
1/2 teaspoon salt
Dash ground white pepper
Sprig of mint or 1 bay leaf for garnish

In a medium serving bowl, lightly toss pineapple and beets. In a small bowl, use a whisk to beat vinegar, oil, sugar, salt and white pepper. Pour dressing over beets and pineapple; toss. Garnish with mint or bay leaf; serve immediately. Makes 6 to 8 servings.

Fish Frikadeller

Fiskefrikadeller—Denmark

"Frikadeller" is almost a synonym for Danish meatballs.

1 lb. fresh or frozen cod or whitefish fillets	1/8 teaspoon ground white pepper
1 small onion, quartered	1/2 teaspoon baking powder
1 teaspoon salt	1 cup milk
1/2 cup all-purpose flour	1 teaspoon curry powder, if desired
1 egg	Butter for frying

Thaw frozen fish. Pat dry with paper towels. Skin and bone fish if necessary; cut fish into several pieces. Grind fish and onion in a food grinder 3 times or until pureed. In a large bowl, combine pureed mixture, salt, flour, egg, white pepper, baking powder, 1/2 cup milk and curry powder, if desired. Beat until blended. Or, fit food processor with steel blade. Turn processor on and drop in fish strips. Process until pureed; add onion and process until minced. Add salt, flour, egg, white pepper, baking powder, 1/2 cup milk and curry powder, if desired. Process until smooth. Spoon mixture into a large bowl. Place over another large bowl filled with crushed ice. Chill, stirring, until mixture thickens. Slowly stir in remaining milk. Cover and chill over ice 20 minutes longer. In a large skillet over medium-low heat, melt enough butter to coat bottom of skillet. Dip 2 tablespoons into ice water until cold. Use cold spoons to shape fish mixture into egg-shape ovals. Fry ovals in butter 4 to 5 minutes on each side. Add more butter as needed. Serve hot. Makes 4 main-dish servings, or about 20 fishballs.

Smoked Farmer's Cheese

Rygeost—Denmark

In Denmark, this caraway-flavored cheese is smoked over a nettle fire.

2 qts. dairy buttermilk	2 tablespoons caraway seeds
1/2 cup whipping cream	Fresh fruit or vegetables
1/2 to 1 teaspoon salt	

Preheat oven to 200F (95C). Pour buttermilk and cream into a 3- or 4-quart casserole dish. Cover and bake 2-1/2 hours or until curds separate from whey. Line a colander or sieve with a damp towel or several layers of damp cheesecloth. Pour mixture through lined colander or sieve. Press to squeeze out as much liquid as possible. Let drain 2 hours. Spoon cheese into a medium bowl. Stir in salt to taste. Rinse out towel or cheesecloth and use to line colander or sieve again. Turn salted mixture into cheesecloth; place over a large bowl. Refrigerate and let drain overnight. Remove cheese from cloth; shape into a ball. Press caraway seeds onto surface of cheese. Place cheese ball in a large metal sieve. Place over a smoking charcoal fire, 10 minutes or until cheese is lightly coated from smoke. Do not burn. Serve immediately or refrigerate until chilled. Serve with fruit or vegetables. Makes about 1/2 pound cheese.

How to Make Fish Frikadeller

1/Puree fish until light and fluffy. Stir in flour, egg, pepper, baking powder, milk and curry powder.

2/Use 2 cold tablespoons to shape chilled mixture into egg-shape ovals. Fry until lightly browned.

Cranberry-Rye Pudding

Ruismarjapuuro—Finland

Finns also like to serve this hot, for breakfast, with a little cream poured over the top.

1 cup rye flour	4 cups cranberry juice
2 tablespoons cornstarch	1/4 cup dark corn syrup
1/2 cup sugar	2 tablespoons sugar
1/2 teaspoon salt	Sweetened whipped cream

In a large saucepan, combine rye flour, cornstarch, 1/2 cup sugar and salt. Stir in cranberry juice and corn syrup. Beat with a whisk until blended. Stirring constantly with whisk, bring to a boil over medium heat. Stirring occasionally, cook until thickened, about 20 minutes. Place over a bowl of ice water. Stir with a whisk until cool, about 10 minutes. Pour into a serving bowl. Sprinkle 2 tablespoons sugar over top. Cover and refrigerate. Serve with whipped cream. Makes 8 servings.

❖ New Year's Eve Smörgåsbord ❖

Many old superstitions and beliefs are connected with New Year's Eve in Scandinavia. Some still feel that herring eaten on this night will bring good fortune. And, if you eat cabbage or sauerkraut, an apple or a bun and a piece of sausage, it will bring good health. Eaten together, it gives the assurance of a good year. Red candles in the candelabra further assure good fortune.

In years past, farmers thought if their cows were in good spirits at the beginning of the new year, the animals would be fruitful during the year. Fruit trees were given an additional winter wrapping to assure a good crop. In reality, the wrapping may have protected the trees from hungry rabbits. Because of the deep snow, by New Year's the rabbits had a firm footing to reach the bark of the tree at a higher level.

It was considered risky to have cracked jars and jugs in the house. As midnight approached, all cracked jars and jugs were broken. It was also believed that the louder the noise made on New Year's, the farther away evil spirits would stay. Therefore, firecrackers were set off and there was much dancing and singing.

Scandinavians also believed that whatever happened on New Year's Day foretold what would happen during the year. Consequently, households were peaceful. People tried not to part with money. In fact, they tried to obtain money. Often, an employee gave his employer a penny to wish him good profits for the coming year.

New Year's Eve, until about 1900, was a time for exchanging small gifts. This was an expression of the wish that the receiver would lack nothing during the coming year.

Today, many families spend New Year's Eve at home telling stories and predicting fortunes. Or, if there are parties, they often include whole families. One popular tradition is to melt small pieces of lead or tin in a heavy iron spoon in the fireplace. The molten metal is poured into a bucket of cold water, making it harden into an unusual shape. The piece is studied. Its shadow cast on a wall is analyzed. Then an older member of the group or a soothsayer friend predicts fortunes for the coming year based on the object's shape and shadow. Fortunes are usually good, causing great excitement among the children.

All Scandinavian countries share the Christmas and New Year's tradition of serving a rice-pudding dessert. A single almond is hidden in the pudding. The person finding the almond is due good luck, has the privilege of handing out gifts, or receives some other special award. Recently, at a Finnish language-and-culture camp in the United States, 85 campers were told about the rice pudding and the significance of the almond. The pudding was served that night. The lucky person was to sing before the entire group. The cook buried an almond in 85 servings. The planners thought there would be a chorus, but not one person admitted finding the almond.

New Year's Eve Smörgåsbord

First Course:
Sherried Herring (Sherrysil), Mustard-Dill Mayonnaise (Laxsas)
Bird's Nests (Linnunpesä)

Cold-Food Course:
Caviar-Stuffed Eggs (Farserede AEg)
Pressed-Beef Roll (Rullepulse), page 52
Herring Salad (Rosolli), Dilled Potato Salad (Potatissallad)
Seafood-Grapefruit Mold (Grapefrugt med Krabbe)

Hot-Food Course:
Fish Mousse (Fiskepudding), page 60, Shrimp Sauce (Rekesaus), page 62
Smorgasbord Meatballs (Små Köttbullar)
Apple-Stuffed Pork Loin (Fylt Svinekam)
Cooked Whole Potatoes

Rye-Meal Bread (Ruisleipä), page 134
White Potato Bread (Potetbrød), page 131

Havarti, Gammelost, Ekte Gjetost Cheeses
Finnish Egg Cheese (Munajuusto)

Dessert Course:
Danish Rum Pudding (Rombudding), Raspberry Sauce (Hindbærsauce)
Finnish Rice Pudding (Riisipuuro), page 45
Almond-Caramel Cake (Toskakake), page 121

Fruit-Juice Glögg (Saft Glögg), page 88
Hot Wine Punch (Glögg)

Apple-Stuffed Pork Loin

Fylt Svinekam — Norway

Fruit holds moisture and makes this roast tender and juicy.

1 (4- to 6-lb.) boneless pork-loin roast
1 green apple, peeled, cored, sliced
10 pitted prunes

1 tablespoon salt
1 teaspoon freshly ground black pepper
3 cups chicken or beef broth, beer or water

Preheat oven to 350F (175C). Lay meat on a flat surface, fat-side down. Arrange apple slices and prunes over surface of roast. Sprinkle with 1 teaspoon salt and 1/2 teaspoon pepper. Tightly roll up roast, enclosing filling. Tie in at least 3 places with kitchen twine. Rub outside of roast with remaining salt and pepper. Place rolled roast in a deep roasting pan. Bake 2-1/2 to 3 hours or until meat is tender when pierced with a fork. Baste every 30 minutes with about 1/2 cup broth, beer or water. Place cooked meat on a hot platter; keep warm. Pour juices from roasting pan through a strainer into a shallow saucepan. Bring to a boil over medium heat. Stirring occasionally, boil until reduced to about 1 cup of shiny glaze. Remove string from roast. Brush roast with glaze. Slice to serve. Makes 8 servings.

Bird's Nests

Linnunpesä—Finland

Sometimes called "ox-eye" because the egg yolks are circled by rings of chopped savory foods.

1 (3-oz.) can Swedish anchovy fillets, chopped
2 tablespoons finely chopped onion
2 tablespoons capers, drained
1/3 cup chopped chives or green-onion tops

1/3 cup minced fresh parsley
1 small potato, cooked, chopped
1/4 cup diced pickled beets
2 unbroken raw egg yolks
Crackers or crisp buttered-toast triangles

Side by side, on center of an oval platter, invert 2 egg cups or small drinking glasses, about 2 inches apart. Arrange anchovies in a ring around cups or glasses. Around anchovies, make a ring of onion, then capers, chives or green-onion tops, parsley, potato and beets. If rings of ingredients are too close to edge of platter, gently move them closer to center of platter. Remove egg cups or glasses; carefully place 1 unbroken raw egg yolk into each open spot. Arrange crackers or toast triangles around edge of platter. The first person to serve himself breaks the egg yolks and mixes the ingredients. Makes about 12 appetizers.

Sherried Herring

Sherrysill—Sweden

The flavor of sherry with herring makes this a delightful dish.

2 salted herring (about 1-1/2 lbs.)
1/2 cup sherry
1/4 cup water
1/4 cup white vinegar

1/2 cup sugar
1/4 teaspoon ground allspice
2 onions, thinly sliced
Chopped fresh dill for garnish

In refrigerator, soak herring overnight in cold water to cover. Drain. Remove head, tail, skin and backbone from fish. Rinse in cold water. Cut herring crosswise into 3/4-inch slices. Place in a medium, nonmetal bowl. Combine sherry, water, vinegar, sugar and allspice. Pour over fish. Top with onions. Cover and refrigerate 24 hours. Drain marinade off herring. Arrange herring and onion rings on a plate; garnish with dill. Makes about 24 herring pieces.

Caviar-Stuffed Eggs   Photo on pages 110-111.

Farserede Æg—Denmark

These are especially pretty when you use both red and black caviar to top the eggs.

4 hard-cooked eggs
1 tablespoon butter, room temperature
1 tablespoon prepared mustard

3 tablespoons red or black caviar
Parsley for garnish

Cut eggs in half lengthwise. Carefully remove egg yolks and place in a small bowl. Use a fork to mash egg yolks and blend in butter and mustard. Press through a small sieve to make smooth. Arrange egg whites, cut-side up, on a platter. Spoon egg-yolk mixture into centers of egg whites. Top each with about 1 teaspoon caviar; garnish with parsley. Makes 8 servings.

How to Make Bird's Nests

1/Arrange ingredients, in order given, around inverted glasses.

2/To serve, break yolk and blend ingredients. Spread on toast.

Seafood-Grapefruit Mold

Grapefrugt med Krabbe—Denmark

Tangy grapefruit flavors the gelatin ring and blends with an elegant crab-salad filling.

1 (16-oz.) can grapefruit segments
1 (1/4-oz.) envelope unflavored gelatin
About 1 cup white wine
1/4 cup whipping cream
1/4 cup mayonnaise

1/2 lb. cooked crabmeat, drained
1 (10-oz.) pkg. frozen asparagus pieces,
    cooked, drained
Lettuce leaves or parsley for garnish

Drain grapefruit, reserving juice in a 2-cup glass measure. Add gelatin to juice; soak 5 minutes. Place over pan of boiling water; stir until gelatin is dissolved. Add white wine to make 2 cups. Place over ice water; chill, stirring, until mixture has consistency of unbeaten egg whites. Pour 1/4 cup mixture into bottom of a 3-cup ring mold. Refrigerate until set, about 20 minutes. Arrange drained grapefruit segments over top; cover with remaining partially set gelatin mixture. Refrigerate until set, about 2 hours. In a medium bowl, beat cream until stiff peaks form; fold in mayonnaise, then crabmeat and asparagus. Invert molded gelatin onto a serving plate; spoon crab salad into center. Garnish with lettuce leaves or parsley. Makes about 6 luncheon servings.

Dilled Potato Salad

Potatissallad—Scandinavia

A natural for the smörgåsbord and for picnics.

Dill Dressing, see below
6 medium potatoes, cooked, chilled,
   peeled, sliced
2 tablespoons chopped green onion

2 tablespoons chopped fresh parsley
1/2 cup diced pickled beets
2 tablespoons chopped chives or
   green-onion tops

Dill Dressing:
2 tablespoons white-wine vinegar
1 teaspoon salt
1/4 teaspoon ground white pepper

1/4 teaspoon dried dill weed or to taste
6 tablespoons vegetable oil

Prepare Dill Dressing; set aside. In a large bowl, combine potatoes, green onion, parsley, **beets** and chives or green-onion tops. Pour dressing over potato mixture; toss to distribute. Refrigerate 30 minutes or until ready to serve. Makes 6 servings.

Dill Dressing:
In a small bowl, combine all ingredients. Beat with a whisk until blended.

Herring Salad   Photo on pages 110-111.

Rosolli—Finland

Almost always found on a smörgåsbord menu, this makes an excellent salad for any meal.

2 cups diced, cooked beets or
   1 (16-oz.) can diced beets
2 medium potatoes, cooked, peeled, diced
2 tart apples, peeled, diced
2 carrots, peeled, cooked, diced

1 small onion, minced
1 dill pickle, diced
1 cup diced pickled herring
Whipped-Cream Dressing, see below

Whipped-Cream Dressing:
1 cup whipping cream
2 tablespoons lemon juice
2 teaspoons beet juice

1/4 teaspoon salt
Sugar to taste

Drain beets, reserving 2 teaspoons juice for dressing. In a large, shallow, serving bowl, arrange potatoes, apples, carrots, onion, pickle and drained beets, side by side in rows. Arrange **herring** around edge of salad. Prepare Whipped-Cream Dressing. Let guests serve themselves, mixing **in**-gredients on their plates. Serve dressing with salad. Makes 8 dinner servings or 16 to 20 **appetizer** servings.

Whipped-Cream Dressing:
In a medium bowl, beat cream until soft peaks form. Fold in remaining ingredients. Spoon **into a** small serving bowl. Makes about 1 cup.

Smörgåsbord Meatballs

Små Köttbullar—Swedish

Meatballs for the smörgåsbord should be about the size of large marbles.

1 tablespoon butter
1 tablespoon minced onion
2/3 cup soft breadcrumbs
1 cup water
3/4 lb. ground lean beef
1/4 lb. ground lean pork

1 teaspoon salt
1/2 teaspoon ground allspice, if desired
1/2 teaspoon ground white pepper
1/2 teaspoon sugar
Butter for frying, melted
1 cup condensed beef consommé

Melt 1 tablespoon butter in a large skillet. Add onion; sauté 1 to 2 minutes until tender. In large bowl of electric mixer, combine breadcrumbs and water; let stand 1 to 2 minutes. Add beef, pork, sautéed onion, salt, allspice, if desired, white pepper and sugar. Beat with electric mixer on low speed until smooth. Turn mixer to high speed. Beat meat mixture until light and fluffy, about 10 minutes. Meat will lighten in color during beating. Dip 2 teaspoons in ice water until cold. Use cold spoons to shape meat into tiny meatballs. Pour melted butter for frying 1/4 inch deep in a large skillet. Place over medium heat. Add meatballs to hot butter. Brown on all sides, constantly shaking pan. Drain on paper towels; keep warm. When all meatballs are browned, pour undiluted consommé into skillet. Bring to a boil, stirring vigorously to scrape up bits of meat from skillet. Stirring constantly, boil until mixture is reduced to a thick, syrupy glaze, 10 to 15 minutes. Arrange hot cooked meatballs in a shallow serving dish. Pour glaze over meatballs. Serve hot. Makes 6 main-dish servings, or about 50 tiny meatballs.

Finnish Egg Cheese   Photo on pages 110-111.

Munajuusto—Finland

This mild-flavored, farm-style cheese is excellent with fresh fruits or berries.

4 eggs
3 cups dairy buttermilk
2 qts. homogenized whole milk

1-1/2 teaspoons salt
1 teaspoon sugar

In a large bowl, beat eggs with a whisk; beat in buttermilk until blended. In a 4-quart saucepan, bring milk to a boil over medium heat. Stirring constantly, slowly add egg mixture and bring mixture to a boil; immediately remove from heat. Curds will separate from whey in about 1 minute, without stirring. Again place over medium heat until mixture comes to a boil. Stir in salt and sugar, then immediately remove from heat. Cover and let stand at room temperature 30 minutes or until curds rise to top of mixture. Line a colander or large sieve with a damp towel or several layers of damp cheesecloth. Place lined colander or sieve over a large bowl. Gently pour curds-and-whey mixture into lined sieve or colander. Let drain 10 minutes. Fold ends of cloth over curds. Gently lift curds in cloth; fit into a cheese mold or any form with drainage holes in bottom, such as a clean flowerpot. Place a weight on top of cloth. Set mold in a dish large enough to catch dippings; refrigerate 24 hours. Discard whey or use to make bread. Remove cheese from mold; unwrap cheese. Serve immediately, or preheat oven to 450F (230C). Place cheese on an ungreased baking sheet; brush with melted butter. Bake 10 to 15 minutes or until browned. Makes 1/2 to 3/4 pound cheese.

Danish Rum Pudding

Photo on pages 110-111.

Rombudding—Denmark

Serve this smooth pudding with Raspberry Sauce, below, or fill the center with fresh berries.

2 (1/4-oz.) envelopes unflavored gelatin	1/4 cup light rum
1/4 cup cold water	1 cup whipping cream, whipped
5 egg yolks	Fresh raspberries or Raspberry Sauce,
3/4 cup sugar	below, if desired
2 cups hot milk	

Lightly oil a 1-1/2-quart fancy dessert mold; set aside. In a small bowl, sprinkle gelatin over water; set aside to soften, 2 to 3 minutes. In top of double boiler or in a large metal bowl, beat egg yolks until frothy. Slowly beat in sugar and milk until light and lemon colored. Place over simmering water. Stirring constantly, cook 10 minutes or until smooth and creamy. Stir in rum, then gelatin mixture. Cover and refrigerate until mixture begins to set, about 45 minutes. Fold in whipped cream. Pour into prepared mold. Refrigerate 4 to 6 hours or until set. Invert onto a serving dish. Serve with raspberries or Raspberry Sauce, if desired. Makes 6 to 8 servings.

Variation

Substitute 1 teaspoon rum extract for rum. Use only 1 (1/4-ounce) envelope unflavored gelatin.

Raspberry Sauce

Photo on pages 110-111.

Hindbærsauce—Denmark

Serve this sauce over rum pudding, cake or ice cream.

1 (10-oz.) pkg. frozen raspberries, thawed	1 tablespoon cornstarch
3/4 cup red-currant jelly	

In a medium saucepan, combine raspberries with juice, jelly and cornstarch. Bring to a boil over medium heat, stirring constantly. Cook and stir until thickened. Cool. Makes 2 cups.

Mustard-Dill Mayonnaise

Laxsås—Scandinavia

Serve this sauce with Gravlax, page 113, or another hot or cold fish.

1/4 cup Dijon-style mustard	2 tablespoons white-wine vinegar
1 teaspoon dry mustard	1/3 cup vegetable oil
3 tablespoons sugar	3 tablespoons minced fresh dill

In a small, deep bowl, combine Dijon-style and dry mustard; blend in sugar and vinegar to make a paste. With a whisk, whip in oil until mixture resembles thick mayonnaise. Stir in dill. Let sauce stand at room temperature 25 minutes to let flavors blend. Makes 1 cup.

Hot Wine Punch

Glögg—Sweden

This spicy wine punch is a wintertime favorite in Scandinavia.

1 medium orange
2 liters dry red wine
2 liters dry white wine
2 cups light or dark raisins
12 whole cardamom pods,
  white part removed, seeds bruised

10 whole cloves
1 (2-inch) piece gingerroot, peeled
1 (3-inch) cinnamon stick
1/4 to 1/2 cup sugar
2 cups whole blanched almonds

Use a vegetable peeler to cut colored peel, or zest, from orange. Be careful not to get any white pith. Use orange for another purpose. In a 6- to 8-quart non-aluminum pot, combine orange peel, wines, raisins, cardamom, cloves, gingerroot and cinnamon stick. Cover and let stand 12 to 24 hours to let flavors blend. Shortly before serving, bring to a simmer over medium heat. Do not boil. Stir in sugar to taste until dissolved. Stir in almonds. Serve hot punch in mugs. Makes 12 to 15 servings.

Variations

For a non-alcoholic punch, substitute white-grape juice or apple cider for wine.

Flaming Glögg: Omit sugar. As wine mixture heats, place about 20 sugar cubes in a sieve; set aside. Pour 1-1/2 cups aquavit, schnapps, rum, brandy or cognac into a small saucepan. Stir over low heat until warmed. Use a long-stemmed match to ignite alcohol. Pour 1/4 cup pearl sugar into a strainer. Holding strainer with sugar over wine mixture, pour flaming beverage over sugar. When flame goes out, stir remaining sugar into punch. Stir in almonds before serving.

To Cook Rice

In a medium saucepan, combine 1 cup rice, 2 cups water and 1 teaspoon salt. Bring to a rolling boil, then lower heat until the water just simmers. Cover and simmer 15 to 20 minutes until the water is absorbed. **To prepare in the microwave**, combine rice, water and salt in a deep, 2-quart glass dish. Cover and microwave at full power, 5 minutes or until mixture boils. Microwave at medium or 50% power, 15 to 20 minutes until water is absorbed.

By rows, starting at top left: Danish Rum Pudding with Raspberry Sauce, page 108; Blueberry Bars, page 153. Second row: Herring Salad, page 106; Carrot Casserole, page 118; Finnish Cucumber Salad, page 94; Herring Fillets, Horseradish Cream Dressing, Sour Cream and Curry-Mayonnaise Dressing, page 114. Third row: Finnish Egg Cheese, page 107; Boneless Birds, page 116; Pressed-Beef Roll, page 52. Fourth row: Rye & Wheat Flatbread, page 31; Mrs. Olson's Flour Lefse, page 124; Danish Pumpernickel, page 135; Salted Salmon, page 113; Caviar-Stuffed Eggs, page 104.

❖ Parent's Day Smörgåsbord ❖

Father's Day was first celebrated in Scandinavia in 1931. On the second Sunday in November, father is usually awakened in the morning with a breakfast tray. It contains his favorite pastry, morning cup of coffee, flowers and a gift. The day centers around father, with everyone thinking of things to make his day special. Dinner includes father's favorite foods, and he invites his favorite friends. Food choices may include a variety of meats and potatoes, but herring, cheese and bread are always on the menu.

Most Scandiavian fathers enjoy salted fish. Salted fish has remained a favorite of Scandinavians from the days when they preserved fish and other meats by salting them. The salting process breaks down the muscle tissues, giving you a tender texture and mild flavor. Salted Salmon is a smörgåsbord favorite. It is used on open-face sandwiches and as appetizers. It is expensive when bought in a store, but is much less expensive when prepared at home by the easy method in my recipe.

Mother's Day is celebrated the last Sunday in May and is an equally good excuse for a special meal. Be sure to plan it so mother can escape the work. Mother's Day became an annual holiday in Sweden in 1919 and is now celebrated in all of Scandinavia. It was borrowed from England where it had existed as *Mothering Sunday* since the 17th Century.

But in 1919, there were problems. Mother was probably the only family member who knew how to plan and carry out a celebration or tradition. Therefore, it was necessary to publish a set of instructions for other family members.

Mors Dag instructions as published in Sweden in 1920:
1. Raise the Flag.
2. Greet Mother with songs in the morning.
3. Serve coffee and coffeecake before she gets out of bed.
4. Give her flowers and a small gift.

In the afternoon, the family takes a torte or cake and a bouquet of spring flowers—primroses or anemones—to Grandmother. The cake is usually fancy, rich and cream-filled such as Strawberry Cream Cake, page 88.

If this is a tradition you want to start in your family, take Grandmother her favorite cake. A young friend of ours has adopted a "grandmother" in a near-by nursing home. She often enjoys gifts such as this.

Long spring days bring all of Scandinavia to an intense and fruitful summer season. The sun doesn't quite set as it skims the horizon at midnight. It forcefeeds the countryside into greenness and gardens into a pageant of flowers. Vegetables and fruits mature early.

In appreciation of springtime after a long winter, Scandinavians place leafy branches from silver birch trees on either side of entrances to buildings, restaurants, apartment buildings, shops and homes. Everywhere you look, doors, decks, gardens, patios—even balconies on high-rise apartment buildings—are decorated with leaves and flowers.

Select and prepare two or more dishes from each course in the menu that follows.

Parent's Day Smörgåsbord

First Course:
Herring Fillets (Sildfiller med Saser)

Cold-Food Course:
Salted Salmon (Gravlax), Veal Terrine (Sylte), page 8
Mushroom Salad (Sienisalaatti), West-Coast Salad (Västkustsallat)

Hot-Food Course:
Spicy Marinated Pork (Stegt Svinekam)
Boneless Birds (Okserulader)
Gingered Brown Beans (Bruna Bönor)
Carrot Casserole (Porkkanalaatikko)
Rutabaga-Potato Casserole (Perunalanttulaatikko)

Danish Pumpernickel (Rugbrød), page 135
Potato Flatbread (Lefse), page 124

Emmentaler, Gjetost, Danablu, Edam Cheeses
Baked Bread Cheese (Leipäjuusto)

Dessert Course:
Finnish Air Pudding (Ilmapuuro)
Veiled Country Lass (Bondepige med Slør)
Blueberry Bars (Mustikkapiirakka), page 153

Red or White Wine, Coffee, Tea

Salted Salmon

Photo on pages 110-111.

Gravlax—Scandinavia

This simple-to-prepare dish is popular in all Scandinavian countries.

2 lbs. fresh salmon fillet	1/4 cup salt
1/2 cup chopped fresh dill or	1/4 cup sugar
2 tablespoons dried dill weed,	1/4 teaspoon ground white pepper
crumbled	1/4 teaspoon ground allspice

Rinse salmon; dry with paper towels. Place in a 13" x 9" glass dish. Sprinkle with half of dill. In a small bowl, combine salt, sugar, white pepper and allspice. Sprinkle half of mixture over fish; turn fish over, sprinkle with remaining salt mixture. Top with remaining dill. Cover with plastic wrap; refrigerate 24 hours. If a compact texture is desired, place a 12" x 7" dish on top of fish. Place several cans of food in top dish for weight. Occasionally spoon juices over fish. To serve, drain fish and cut diagonally in 1/8-inch slices. Arrange on a platter. Makes 12 appetizer servings.

Herring Fillets   Photo on pages 110-111.

Sildfiller med Saser—Scandinavia

This herring is delectable with or without the sauces.

1 lb. salted or brined herring
Horseradish Sauce, see below
Curry-Mayonnaise Sauce, see below

1/4 cup chopped fresh chives
1/4 cup chopped green onion, with tops
1 cup dairy sour cream

Horseradish Sauce:
1/2 cup whipping cream
1/4 teaspoon lemon juice

1/8 teaspoon sugar
2 tablespoons grated fresh horseradish

Curry-Mayonnaise Sauce:
1/2 cup mayonnaise
1/4 cup whipping cream, whipped
1/2 teaspoon curry powder

1/4 teaspoon paprika
1/2 teaspoon dried dill weed, crumbled
1/2 teaspoon dried leaf oregano, crumbled

In refrigerator, soak herring overnight in cold water to cover. Prepare Horseradish Sauce and Curry-Mayonnaise Sauce, 1 or 2 hours before serving. Drain fish; remove head, tail, skin and backbone. Rinse in cold water. Cut fish crosswise into 3/4-inch slices. Arrange herring slices on a serving tray or board. Place chopped chives, chopped green onion and sour cream in separate small bowls. Let guests spoon a sauce or sour cream over top. Garnish with chives or green onion. Makes 16 to 20 herring pieces.

Horseradish Cream Dressing:
In a small bowl, whip cream until soft peaks form. Stir in remaining ingredients. Makes 3/4 cup.

Curry-Mayonnaise Dressing:
In a small bowl, blend all ingredients. Makes 1 cup.

Gingered Brown Beans

Bruna Bönor—Sweden

This traditional Swedish brown-bean dish has a pleasant sweet-sour flavor.

2 cups Swedish brown beans or pinto beans
5 cups water
1 teaspoon salt
2 teaspoons chopped crystallized ginger
1/4 cup cider vinegar

1/4 cup dark corn syrup
1/4 cup packed brown sugar
1 teaspoon ground ginger
Salt, vinegar and corn syrup, if desired

Rinse and pick over beans. Place in a large saucepan with water and 1 teaspoon salt. Let stand overnight. Retaining water beans were soaked in, bring to a boil over medium-high heat. Add crystallized ginger. Cover and simmer over low heat 1-1/2 hours or until beans are tender. Use a potato masher to crush some of beans. Stir in 1/4 cup vinegar, 1/4 cup syrup, brown sugar and ground ginger. Simmer 30 minutes longer or until thickened. Taste and add more salt, vinegar and syrup, if desired. Makes 6 to 8 servings.

Rutabaga-Potato Casserole
Perunalanttulaatikko—Finland

Photo on pages 46-47.

This casserole can be assembled a day in advance and baked just before serving.

2 lbs. rutabagas or turnips, peeled, diced
1/2 lb. potatoes, peeled, diced
4 cups water
1/3 cup all-purpose flour
1/2 cup soft breadcrumbs
1/3 cup whipping cream
1/3 cup dark corn syrup
1/4 cup butter, melted

2 eggs, beaten
1 teaspoon salt
1/2 teaspoon ground allspice
1/2 teaspoon ground nutmeg
1/2 teaspoon ground ginger
1/4 teaspoon ground white pepper
2 to 3 tablespoons butter, melted

In a large saucepan, combine rutabagas or turnips and potatoes; add water. Bring to a boil; cook over low heat 25 minutes or until tender. Drain, reserving cooking liquid. Mash rutabagas or turnips and potatoes until smooth. Butter a shallow 2-quart casserole dish; set aside. Preheat oven to 300F (150C). In large bowl of electric mixer, beat potato mixture on high speed, adding 1/2 cup cooking liquid during beating. Beat in flour, breadcrumbs, cream, syrup, 1/4 cup melted butter, eggs, salt, allspice, nutmeg, ginger and white pepper. Beat until light and fluffy. Spoon into prepared casserole dish. Use a spoon to smooth top. Drizzle with 2 to 3 tablespoons melted butter. Bake, uncovered, 1-1/2 to 2 hours or until surface is lightly browned. Makes 8 servings.

West-Coast Salad
Västkustsallat—Sweden

Photo on cover.

A must for the smörgåsbord table; also serve this beautiful salad for lunch or supper.

Garlic Dressing, see below
Crisp lettuce leaves
1 lb. fresh asparagus,
  cut in 1-inch pieces, cooked
1/2 lb. mushrooms, sliced
1 (16-oz.) can beets, cut in
  julienne pieces

1 cup frozen baby peas, thawed
3 tomatoes, cut in wedges
3 hard-cooked eggs, quartered
1 cup cooked tiny shrimp
2 (6-oz.) pkgs. frozen crabmeat,
  thawed, drained
3 tablespoons minced fresh parsley

Garlic Dressing:
2 garlic cloves, minced or mashed
2 teaspoons Dijon-style mustard
2 tablespoons white-wine vinegar

1/4 cup olive or vegetable oil
3 tablespoons minced fresh dill

Prepare Garlic Dressing; set aside. Line a large shallow bowl or platter with lettuce leaves. Over lettuce, arrange asparagus, mushrooms, beets, peas, tomatoes, eggs, shrimp and crabmeat. Sprinkle with parsley. Serve immediately with Garlic Dressing. Makes 8 luncheon servings.

Garlic Dressing:
In a medium bowl, combine garlic, mustard and vinegar. Use a whisk to beat in oil until dressing is thick. Fold in dill.

Boneless Birds

Photo on pages 110-111.

Okserulader—Norway

Stuffed-and-rolled meat is a favorite in all the Scandinavian countries.

2 lbs. beef round steak, sliced 1/4 inch thick	2 tablespoons chopped parsley
1 teaspoon salt	1 small onion, sliced lengthwise
1/2 teaspoon ground allspice	2 tablespoons all-purpose flour
1/4 lb. mushrooms, chopped	2 tablespoons butter
1/4 lb. bacon, diced	1/2 cup beef broth
	1/2 cup half and half

Cut meat into 8 equal pieces. Place between pieces of plastic wrap. With flat side of a meat mallet, pound until meat is thin and almost doubled in size. Sprinkle flattened meat with salt and allspice. Evenly spoon mushrooms, bacon, parsley and onion on top of seasoned meat pieces. Roll up tightly, jelly-roll fashion, and secure with wooden picks or tie with cotton string. Roll meat rolls in flour. Melt butter in a large, heavy skillet over medium heat. Add meat rolls; brown on all sides. As rolls are browned, place in an oven-to-table casserole dish. Preheat oven to 300F (150C). Add broth and half and half to drippings in skillet; stir over medium-low heat until thickened. Pour over meat rolls. Cover and bake 1 hour or until meat is tender. Makes 8 servings.

Spicy Marinated Pork

Stegt Svinekam—Denmark

In Scandinavia, fresh juniper berries are picked from cedar trees.

1 (4- to 6-lb.) boneless pork-loin roast, rolled, tied	1 tablespoon ground allspice
1-1/2 cups red port wine	1 tablespoon ground ginger
1/2 cup red-wine vinegar	1 teaspoon salt
1 tablespoon juniper berries or whole allspice	1/2 cup whipping cream
	2 tablespoons crumbled blue cheese (1/2 oz.)
	2 tablespoons red-currant or wild-plum jelly

Wipe meat with paper towels to remove moisture; set aside. In a large, deep nonmetal bowl, combine wine, vinegar, juniper berries or whole allspice, ground allspice, ginger and salt. Add meat, turning several times to coat evenly. Cover and refrigerate at least 6 hours or overnight, turning once or twice. To bake, 3-1/2 to 4 hours before serving, preheat oven to 325F (165C). Remove meat from marinade. Insert a meat thermometer into center of roast. Place on a rack in a medium roasting pan. Pour marinade into bottom of pan. Bake until thermometer registers 170F (75C), about 3 hours. Baste 3 or 4 times during roasting. Place meat on a hot platter; keep warm. To make a sauce, skim fat from pan drippings. Pour drippings through a strainer into a medium saucepan. Bring drippings to a boil over high heat; stir in cream. Reduce heat until mixture boils gently. Stirring occasionally, boil until liquid is reduced to 1-1/2 cups. Stir in blue cheese and jelly. Beat gently with a whisk until dissolved. Pour sauce into a medium serving bowl. To serve, slice roast; spoon sauce over individual servings. Makes 8 servings.

How to Make Boneless Birds

1/With flat side of a meat mallet, pound meat until thin and about doubled in size.

2/Add mushrooms, bacon, parsley and onion. Roll up tightly; secure with cotton string or wooden picks.

Mushroom Salad

Sienisalaatti—Finland

Finns make this salad with wild mushrooms when they are in season.

1 lb. mushrooms, thinly sliced	**1 teaspoon salt**
2 tablespoons grated onion	**1/8 teaspoon ground white pepper**
2 tablespoons lemon juice	**1/8 teaspoon ground allspice**
2 teaspoons sugar	**Crisp lettuce leaves**
1/2 teaspoon freshly ground black pepper	**1 tomato, cut in wedges**
1/2 cup whipping cream	**Fresh dill or parsley sprigs for garnish**
1/4 cup dairy sour cream	

In a large bowl, combine mushrooms, onion, lemon juice, sugar and black pepper. In a small bowl, beat whipping cream until soft peaks form. Fold in sour cream, salt, white pepper and allspice. Fold cream mixture into mushroom mixture. Line salad platter or bowl with lettuce leaves. Add mushroom mixture; garnish with tomato wedges and dill or parsley sprigs. Makes 8 servings.

Carrot Casserole
Photo on pages 110-111.

Porkkanalaatikko—Finland

This is nutritious enough to be a main dish for a meatless meal.

1 cup cooked rice	1 tablespoon brown sugar
2 cups milk	2 eggs, slightly beaten
4 cups shredded peeled carrots	3 tablespoons butter
1 teaspoon salt	1/3 cup fine dry breadcrumbs

Butter a 2-quart casserole dish; set aside. Preheat oven to 375F (190C). In a large bowl, combine rice, milk, carrots, salt, brown sugar and eggs. Pour into prepared casserole dish. Melt butter in a small skillet; stir in breadcrumbs. Sprinkle buttered crumbs over top of casserole. Bake 45 minutes or until set and carrots are tender. Makes 4 to 8 servings.

Baked Bread Cheese

Leipäjuusto—Finland

This flat, baked cheese resembles a pizza in size and shape.

4 qts. homogenized whole milk	2 teaspoons sugar
1 rennet tablet	Bread
1/4 cup cold water	Cloudberry jam or berries
1 teaspoon coarse kosher salt	

Pour milk into a 6-quart saucepan. Attach a candy thermometer to side of pan with bulb in milk. Place pan over low heat; slowly heat milk to 100F (40C). Maintain this temperature while making cheese. Add rennet to water; stir until dissolved. Stir into heated milk. Cover and let stand 30 minutes or until curd comes away from side of pan when pan is tilted, and curd splits in a straight line when cut with a knife. Stir; cover and let stand 1 hour longer. Line a large colander or sieve with a damp towel or several layers of damp cheesecloth; place over a large bowl. Pour curds and whey into lined colander. Let drain 1 hour or until whey no longer drips from bottom of colander. Butter a 12- to 14-inch pizza pan with raised side. Pat drained curds into pizza pan. Place pizza pan on a baking sheet with raised sides. Elevate 1 side of pizza pan to let whey drain into baking sheet. Preheat broiler. Sprinkle top of cheese with 1/2 teaspoon kosher salt and 1 teaspoon sugar. Broil 8 inches from heat until browned in spots on top of cheese, 25 to 30 minutes. Pour excess whey from baking sheet; wipe baking sheet with a clean damp cloth. Invert cheese onto cleaned baking sheet. Sprinkle with remaining salt and sugar. Return to broiler; broil until browned in spots and cheese is 1/4- to 1/2-inch thick. Cool; cut in wedges. Serve on bread with cloudberry jam or with berries. Makes one 12- to 14-inch bread cheese.

If your mid-winter carrots are pale, add about 1 tablespoon sugar to the cooking water to bring out a brighter color.

Veiled Country Lass

Bondepige med Slør — Denmark

Layers of rye breadcrumbs, applesauce, raspberry jam, chocolate and whipped cream—yum!

2 tablespoons butter
1 cup dry rye breadcrumbs or
   dry chocolate-cake crumbs
2 tablespoons sugar

1/2 cup raspberry jam
3 cups chunk-style applesauce
1/2 cup grated sweet chocolate
1 cup whipping cream, softly whipped

Melt butter in a small skillet over medium heat. Stir in breadcrumbs or cake crumbs and sugar until crumbs are crisp and completely buttered. Spoon one-third of crumb mixture into bottom of a glass serving bowl. Add one-third of the raspberry jam in small dollops. Over jam, spread a layer of about one-third each of the applesauce, chocolate and whipped cream. Repeat layering, saving a little chocolate to sprinkle over top layer of whipped cream to make a fine *veil*. Refrigerate until ready to serve. Makes 6 to 8 servings.

Finnish Air Pudding

Ilmapuuro — Finland

This old-time Finnish favorite is simple and spectacular.

3 cups cranberry juice
6 tablespoons sugar
Pinch salt

1/2 cup uncooked farina or Cream of Wheat
About 1 cup half and half

In a large saucepan, combine cranberry juice, sugar, salt and farina or Cream of Wheat. Stirring constantly, bring to a boil over medium heat. Cook and stir 8 minutes or until thickened. Pour into large bowl of electric mixer. Beat 15 minutes at highest speed. Pudding will become pale pink and volume will increases to about 4 times the original. Pour into a serving bowl; serve immediately. Or, refrigerate until ready to serve. Spoon about 2 tablespoons half and half over each serving. Makes 8 servings.

Low-Calorie Whipped Topping

Combine 1/2 cup nonfat dry milk and 1/3 cup ice water in a deep, medium bowl. Beat with an electric mixer until mixture is thick and stands in soft peaks. Add 1 tablespoon lemon juice. Continue beating until stiff peaks form. Sweeten to taste.

SPECIALTY BAKING

Twice-baked breads, rusks and toasts are found in abundance throughout Scandinavia. You see them in glass jars or bins in bread shops where they can be purchased by the kilo. It is a sensible way to store bread, especially in the summertime when it may be too warm to use the oven. Rusk-making was a Saturday activity in country homes. Breads left from the previous week's baking were sliced and dried in the oven, making pale, dry toast that kept well in an airtight container. Breadmaking usually occurred on Saturday and there would be fresh bread and fresh toast for the following week. Toast made from sweet yeast bread is often dunked in coffee. Rusks are eaten for breakfast, snacks and lunch.

Hardtack, crisp bread and flatbread were also kept in airtight containers during the summer. One Norwegian grandmother told me she made her flour lefse, wrapped it in waxed paper and kept it in a box under her bed. Hardtack and crisp breads resemble crackers. They are excellent eaten with a spread of butter or a simple topping of cheese or cold cuts. Flour lefse is not usually served crisp, but is dipped in hot water, then placed between cloths or towels until soft and pliable. Then it is buttered, sprinkled with sugar or cinnamon-sugar, rolled or folded and cut into bite-size pieces. Potato lefse does not become crisp when cooked, but resembles a thin Mexican flour tortilla. Potato lefse can be prepared several weeks ahead, wrapped airtight and stored in the freezer. Unwrap it to thaw.

Lingonberry Spice Cake

Pepperkake—Norway

Lingonberries or cranberries give this pound cake a gentle tartness.

3/4 cup butter, room temperature
1-1/4 cups granulated sugar
4 eggs
2 teaspoons ground cinnamon
1 teaspoon ground ginger
1 teaspoon ground cloves
2 teaspoons baking powder
1 teaspoon baking soda

1 teaspoon salt
3 cups all-purpose flour
1-1/2 cups dairy sour cream
2 to 4 tablespoons fresh or canned whole
    lingonberries, drained, or
    chopped fresh cranberries
2 to 3 tablespoons powdered sugar

Preheat oven to 350F (175C). Butter a 10-cup Bundt pan. Dust mold lightly with flour. In large bowl of electric mixer, cream butter and granulated sugar until smooth. Beat in eggs until light and fluffy. In a medium bowl, stir together cinnamon, ginger, cloves, baking powder, baking soda, salt and flour. Alternately stir flour mixture and sour cream into sugar mixture until smooth. Fold in lingonberries or cranberries. Pour into prepared Bundt pan. Bake about 55 minutes or until a skewer inserted into cake comes out clean. Invert onto a rack; remove pan. Cool, then dust with powdered sugar. Makes about 12 servings.

Almond-Caramel Cake

Toskakake—Norway

Crunchy, almond topping coats this rich cake.

1 cup whipping cream
2 eggs
1 teaspoon vanilla extract
1-1/2 cups all-purpose flour

1 cup sugar
2 teaspoons baking powder
1/2 teaspoon salt
Caramel Topping, see below

Caramel Topping:
1/3 cup butter
1/3 cup sugar
3/4 cup chopped almonds

1 tablespoon all-purpose flour
1 tablespoon whipping cream

Preheat oven to 350F (175C). Butter a 10-inch springform pan or tart pan with a removable bottom; set aside. In large bowl of electric mixer, beat cream until stiff; beat in eggs and vanilla. In a small bowl, stir together flour, sugar, baking powder and salt. Beat flour mixture into cream mixture until smooth. Pour into prepared pan. Bake 40 minutes or until cake pulls away from side of pan. Prepare Caramel Topping. Pour hot topping over hot cake, completely covering top. Bake 15 to 20 minutes longer or until golden brown. Serve warm or cold. Makes 8 to 10 servings.

Caramel Topping:
Melt butter in a small saucepan over medium heat. Add remaining ingredients. Stirring constantly, bring to a boil. Continue stirring until slightly thickened, 3 to 5 minutes.

Danish Pancake Balls

AEbleskiver—Denmark

These pancake balls are sometimes called "munk," and are eaten as doughnuts.

1/2 cup butter, melted	2 teaspoons baking powder
3 eggs, separated	1/2 teaspoon salt
1 cup milk	1/2 teaspoon ground cardamom, if desired
2 tablespoons sugar	Powdered sugar
1-1/2 cups all-purpose flour	Butter for pan

In a large bowl, blend 1/2 cup melted butter, egg yolks, milk and sugar. In a medium bowl, combine flour, baking powder, salt and cardamom, if desired. Stir into egg-yolk mixture. In a clean medium bowl, beat egg whites until stiff but not dry. Fold into flour mixture. Heat *æbleskiver pan*, page 7, over medium-low heat until a drop of water sizzles when dropped into pan. Spoon 1/2 teaspoon butter into each cup; let melt. Spoon 1 rounded tablespoon batter into each cup. Cook about 1 minute on each side, using a knitting needle or long wooden skewer to turn balls. If heat is too high, centers will be doughy. Dust each with powdered sugar. Serve hot. Makes 20 pancake balls.

Variation

Filled AEbleskiver: Spoon 1 teaspoon applesauce onto center of uncooked batter in each cup. Top with about 1/2 teaspoon additional batter to enclose applesauce. Cook as directed above.

Cream Twists

Kringler—Norway

Not a cookie, bread or cake, but a favorite pastry, buttered and served warm with coffee.

1 cup sugar	1 teaspoon salt
1 egg	2 teaspoons baking powder
1 cup whipping cream	1 teaspoon vanilla extract
1 cup dairy sour cream	3-1/2 cups all-purpose flour

In a large bowl, combine sugar, egg and whipping cream; beat until light and fluffy. Add sour cream, salt, baking powder and vanilla; beat again until light and fluffy. Slowly stir in flour, making a stiff dough. Turn out onto a lightly floured board. Knead only long enough to make a smooth ball. Wrap in plastic wrap; refrigerate overnight. Preheat oven to 450F (230C). Lightly grease a large baking sheet; set aside. Turn out dough onto a lightly floured board. Cut into fourths. Refrigerate 3 portions. Cut remaining portion into 12 equal pieces. Roll each piece between your hands to make an 8-inch rope. Shape each into a figure *8*. Pinch ends to seal. Arrange shaped dough, 2 inches apart, on prepared baking sheet. Bake 6 to 8 minutes or until lightly browned. Cool slightly. Repeat with remaining dough. Place warm rolls in a container with a tight cover to keep them soft and puffy. Wipe moisture from inside of lid as it gathers, so rolls do not become wet. Freeze, if desired. Serve warm. Makes 48 rolls.

Mrs. Olson's Flour Lefse

Photo on pages 110-111.

Nordlenning Krinelefse—Norway

Dry flour lefse is dipped in water to soften before it is served.

2 cups milk
1/4 cup vegetable shortening or lard
1 teaspoon salt
2 cups all-purpose flour

Egg Glaze, page 132
Soft butter
Sugar, if desired
Cinnamon, if desired

In a medium saucepan, bring milk to a boil with shortening or lard and salt. Add flour all at once and stir until very thick. Mixture will resemble cream-puff paste. Remove from heat and cool. Mixture should be very thick but pliable. Divide into fourths. Divide each into 4 equal parts, making 16 pieces. Shape each into a ball, then flatten slightly. Preheat a griddle to 375F (190C). On a lightly floured board, roll 1 ball of dough at a time to a paper-thin 10- or 11-inch circle. Use a grooved *lefse rolling pin,* page 7, to get authentic grid-like texture. Bake dough circles on ungreased preheated griddle, 1 to 2 minutes on each side until browned in spots. Lefse will look dry, but will be flexible, not dry and crisp. Stack baked lefse on a square of waxed paper. Prepare Egg Glaze. When all lefse are baked, brush them, 1 at a time, with glaze. Again place each on griddle, glazed-side up; bake until glaze is dry. Again stack on waxed paper, glazed-side down. **To serve immediately,** brush with soft butter; sprinkle with sugar and cinnamon, if desired. Roll up and cut diagonally into 2-inch slices. Arrange on a bread tray. **To serve later,** store in a cool dry place, loosely wrapped in waxed paper. Lefse will become dry and crisp. Before serving, dip quickly into hot water and stack between cloths or sheets of plastic wrap until soft. Brush with soft butter; sprinkle with sugar and cinnamon, if desired. Roll and cut as directed above, or fold in half and cut into wedges or 2-inch slices. Makes 16 lefse.

Oatmeal Hardtack

Knäckebröd—Sweden

Serve these tender, crisp crackers with cheese and soup.

1/2 cup vegetable shortening
1/4 cup butter, room temperature
1/2 cup sugar
2 cups uncooked rolled oats

3 cups all-purpose flour
1-1/2 teaspoons salt
1 teaspoon baking soda
1-1/2 cups buttermilk

In a large bowl, cream shortening, butter and sugar until smooth. In a medium bowl, combine oats, flour, salt and baking soda. Alternately add flour mixture and buttermilk to creamed mixture, blending until stiff like a cookie dough. Refrigerate 30 minutes. Grease a large baking sheet; sprinkle with rolled oats. Preheat oven to 325F (165C). Divide dough into 8 equal portions. Shape each portion into a smooth ball. Return 7 balls of dough to bowl; cover and refrigerate. Place remaining ball of dough on prepared baking sheet. Flatten as much as possible with your hands, then use a rolling pin to roll dough to edges of baking sheet. Using a *hardtack rolling pin,* page 7, make pebbled imprints on top, or prick evenly with tines of a fork to make a rough texture. Use a pastry wheel, knife or pizza cutter to score dough in 2-inch squares. Bake 15 to 20 minutes or until crisp and golden. Cool 3 minutes on baking sheet, then place on a rack to finish cooling. Break into crackers where scored. Repeat with remaining dough. Makes about 128 crackers.

Loaves of bread or individual rolls can be freshened by quickly dipping them into and out of cold water, them bake them in a preheated 350F (175C) oven 10 minutes.

How to Make Mrs. Olson's Flour Lefse

1/Roll out dough until paper-thin. Use grooved *lefse rolling pin* to make grid-like texture.

2/Lift dough with a thin pointed stick or handle of a wooden spoon. Place on a hot, dry griddle.

3/Bake until lightly browned. Brush 1 side with glaze. Bake, glaze-side up, until dry.

4/Before serving, dip dry lefse in hot water. Wrap to soften. Top with butter and sugar, then roll and cut.

SCANDINAVIAN YEAST BREADS

Visitors to Scandinavia are overwhelmed with the breads. There are dark rye breads, whole-wheat breads, white breads and multiple-grain breads. There are fat loaves, thin loaves, round loaves, crisp breads, flatbreads, buns, rusks and sweet breads. They are the heaviest and the most delicious breads I have ever eaten!

Rye, barley and oats are the grains native to the area. They are quick-growing and mature early in the intensity of long, sunny, summer days. For centuries these grains have been used in the breads of Scandinavia. Some wheat is grown in Sweden and Denmark, but most is imported.

There is a difference between *rye meal* and *rye flour* called for in the following recipes. Rye meal is also called *pumpernickel rye, dark rye* or *coarse rye*. Rye meal contains bran. Rye flour is usually labeled *light rye* or *medium rye*. When making breads that call for rye flour, either light or medium is suitable. It is possible to interchange rye flour and rye meal, but the texture will be different.

Soured-rye loaves have played an important part in bread baking. Years ago, salt was an expensive imported seasoning and sourdough starter was the only yeast available. Because of its tangy flavor, sourdough bread needs very little salt. Thus, soured-rye bread was the answer. Part of the dough was saved each time as a starter for the next batch of bread. Or, dough was mixed in a large wooden bowl that was not washed between bakings. The sourdough starter was saved in dry, crusty pieces of dough left in the bowl.

The custom of baking breads and cookies in animal shapes, especially at Christmastime, goes back to pagan days. It was a ritual to burn offerings to the gods. Scandinavian farmers were too poor to offer their livestock. Instead, their burnt offerings were goats made of straw and breads and small cakes, shaped as animals. Straw goats, called *julbock,* are a popular Christmas ornament today. You can buy some very tiny ones, or those that stand over 18 inches tall.

Scandinavians excel in baking. They use lots of butter, eggs and milk, so their baked goods are some of the best in the world. Today, homemakers are not tied to their ovens. There is a wide variety of excellent breads in bakeries, supermarkets and in open-market squares throughout Scandinavia. One of the most colorful places to shop for breads and pastries is in the open-market square, which exists in most towns. Here, you will meet women who begin their day early, baking the goods they later sell to the public. Sometimes the breads and pastries are still warm.

St. Lucia Saffron Bread   Photo on page 137.

Saffransbröd—Sweden

On December 13th, a girl is named "Lucia" at home or school and serves this bread.

1 (1/4-oz.) envelope active dry yeast	1/2 cup golden raisins
1/4 cup warm water (110F, 45C)	2 eggs, slightly beaten
3/4 cup milk	3-1/2 to 4 cups all-purpose or bread flour
1 teaspoon saffron threads or	Egg Glaze, page 132
1/16 teaspoon powdered saffron	1/4 cup sliced almonds
1/2 cup butter	1/4 cup pearl sugar, page 8, or
1/2 cup sugar	coarsely crushed sugar cubes
1 teaspoon salt	About 1/2 cup raisins for St. Lucia Cats

In a small bowl, stir yeast into warm water; let stand 5 minutes to soften. In a small saucepan, combine milk and saffron. Bring to a boil over medium heat, stirring until milk turns a deep yellow. Pour through a strainer into a large bowl. Stir in butter, sugar, salt and golden raisins. Cool slightly; stir in yeast mixture and eggs. Beating to keep mixture smooth, stir in enough flour to make a stiff dough. Turn out onto a lightly floured board. Cover with a dry cloth; let stand 5 to 15 minutes. Wash and grease bowl; set aside. Grease a large baking sheet; set aside. Adding flour as needed to prevent sticking, knead dough until smooth, about 10 minutes. Place in greased bowl, turning to grease all sides. Cover and let rise in a warm place until doubled in bulk, about 2 hours. Punch down dough; turn out onto a lightly oiled surface. Shape into a Candle Wreath or Lucia Cats, see below. Place shaped dough on prepared baking sheet; let rise in a warm place until doubled in bulk, about 1 hour. Preheat oven to 375F (190C). Brush tops of raised dough with Egg Glaze. Sprinkle with sliced almonds and pearl sugar or crushed sugar cubes. Bake 20 to 25 minutes or until lightly browned; do not overbake. Cool on a rack. Decorate St. Lucia Cats as pictured on page 137. Makes 1 St. Lucia Candle Wreath or about 20 St. Lucia Cats.

Shape Variations

St. Lucia Candle Wreath: Divide dough into 3 equal pieces. Roll each piece between palms of your hands and lightly floured surface to make ropes, 30 inches long. Braid ropes together. Cut about 2 inches or 1/2 cup dough from each end of braid. Place braid on prepared baking sheet, curving into a wreath. Pinch ends together. Shape reserved dough into a rope about 18 inches long. Tie into a bow. Place bow over seam in wreath. Proceed as directed above.

St. Lucia Cats: Divide dough into 5 equal portions. Divide each portion into 4 equal pieces. Roll each piece between palms of your hands to make 6-inch ropes, about 1/2 inch thick. Shape each into a letter *S,* coiling ends in spirals. Lay 1 shaped rope across another, with center of top rope touching center of bottom rope. All spirals will curve in same direction. Press 1 raisin into center of each spiral. Let raise until doubled. Brush with Egg Glaze. Sprinkle with pearl sugar. Bake as directed above.

Saffron gives some Scandinavian yeast breads a special flavor and yellow color, but it is expensive. To give a yellow color, substitute ground turmeric for the saffron. Add nutmeg or cardamom for a different but pleasant flavor.

Shrove Tuesday Buns

Semlor—Sweden

These stuffed buns are usually served in a bowl of hot milk, but I prefer Hot Vanilla Sauce, below.

1 (1/4-oz.) envelope active dry yeast
1/4 cup warm water (110F, 43C)
1 egg
2/3 cup milk, scalded, cooled
1/4 cup granulated sugar
1/2 teaspoon salt
1/2 teaspoon ground cardamom or
    ground cinnamon

1/2 cup butter, softened
2-3/4 to 3 cups all-purpose flour
Egg Glaze, page 132
8 oz. almond paste
1/2 cup whipping cream, whipped
2 tablespoons powdered sugar
Powdered sugar
Double recipe Hot Vanilla Sauce, below

In a large bowl, stir yeast into water. Let stand 5 minutes to soften. Beat in egg, milk, granulated sugar, salt, cardamom or cinnamon and butter. Add 2 cups flour. Beat until smooth and satiny. Add enough of remaining flour to make a stiff dough. Turn out onto a lightly floured board. Cover with a dry cloth; let rest 15 minutes. Clean and lightly oil bowl; set aside. Knead dough 10 minutes or until smooth and satiny. Place in oiled bowl, turning to coat all sides. Cover with dry cloth. Let rise in a warm place until doubled in bulk, about 1 hour. Lightly grease a large baking sheet. Preheat oven to 400F (205C). Turn out dough onto a lightly oiled board. Divide dough into fourths. Divide each fourth into 4 parts. Shape each piece of dough into a round bun, about 1 inch high. Place on prepared baking sheet. Let rise until doubled, 45 to 60 minutes. Brush Egg Glaze over top of risen buns. Bake glazed buns 10 to 12 minutes or until golden brown. Cool on a rack. Cut almond paste into 16 slices. About 1/3 from top, cut horizontally almost through bun, leaving slice attached at 1 side. Insert a slice of almond paste. In a medium bowl, whip cream until soft peaks form; fold in 2 tablespoons powdered sugar. Spoon whipped cream into buns until each is filled and holds top slice open. Or, pipe whipped cream into buns through a pastry bag. Sprinkle powdered sugar over filling and bun. Prepare Hot Vanilla Sauce. To serve, spoon Hot Vanilla Sauce evenly into 16 dessert dishes; place a filled bun on top of sauce. Unfilled buns may be frozen. To serve, thaw and fill. Makes 16 buns.

Hot Vanilla Sauce

Vaniljesås—Sweden

Use this sauce in place of whipped cream on fruit, pie or cake or with Shrove Tuesday Buns, above.

1/4 cup all-purpose flour
1/8 teaspoon salt
1/4 cup sugar

4 cups milk
2 teaspoons vanilla extract
1 tablespoon butter

In a medium saucepan, combine flour, salt and sugar. Slowly stir in milk. Stirring constantly, bring to a boil over medium heat. Cook and stir until thickened. Stir in vanilla and butter until butter melts. Serve hot. Makes 4 cups.

It is easier to shape yeast doughs into ropes or balls if you work on a lightly oiled surface rather than a flour-dusted surface.

How to Make Shrove Tuesday Buns

1/About 1/3 from top, cut a slice almost through bun. Leave 1 side attached. Add almond paste and filling.

2/Sprinkle with powdered sugar. To serve, spoon Hot Vanilla Sauce into dishes. Place filled bun in sauce.

Graham Rusks

Kavring—Norway

In Norway, these twice-baked buns are served for breakfast, or topped with cheese for lunch.

1 (1/4-oz.) envelope active dry yeast	3 tablespoons sugar
2 cups warm water (110F, 45C)	1 teaspoon salt
3 tablespoons lard or vegetable shortening, melted	2 cups graham flour or whole-wheat flour
	2 to 2-1/2 cups all-purpose or bread flour

In a large bowl, stir yeast into warm water; let stand 5 minutes to soften. Stir in lard or shortening, sugar, salt and graham flour or whole-wheat flour. Beat until smooth. Stir in enough all-purpose or bread flour to make a stiff dough. Turn out onto a lightly floured board. Cover with a dry cloth; let stand 5 to 15 minutes. Wash and grease bowl; set aside. Knead dough until smooth, about 10 minutes. Place in greased bowl, turning to grease all sides. Cover and let rise in a warm place until doubled in bulk, about 2 hours. Grease 2 large baking sheets; set aside. Punch down dough; turn out onto a lightly oiled surface. Cut dough in half; divide each half into 12 pieces. Shape each piece into a round ball, 2-1/2 inches in diameter. Arrange buns on prepared baking sheets, about 2 inches apart. Cover and let rise until doubled in bulk, about 45 minutes. Preheat oven to 425F (220C). Bake buns 12 to 15 minutes or until golden brown. Cool on racks. When buns are cooled, split horizontally, using 2 forks to pull buns apart. Reduce oven heat to 250F (120C). Place split buns on baking sheets, split-side up; bake until completely dry, 1 hour. Makes 48 rusks.

Cinnamon Coffee Ring

Kaffekrans—Norway

This no-knead yeast coffeecake is simple, quick and delicious.

1 (1/4-oz.) envelope active dry yeast
1 teaspoon sugar
1/4 cup warm water (110F, 45C)
1 cup milk, scalded, cooled
1/4 cup butter, melted
1/3 cup sugar

1-1/2 teaspoons salt
2-1/2 to 3 cups all-purpose flour
1/4 cup butter, room temperature
1/2 cup sugar
1 tablespoon ground cinnamon
Powdered-Sugar Glaze, if desired, see below

Powdered-Sugar Glaze:
1/2 cup powdered sugar
1 to 2 tablespoons hot coffee or water

In a large bowl, stir yeast and 1 teaspoon sugar into warm water; let stand 5 minutes to soften. Stir in milk, 1/4 cup melted butter, 1/3 cup sugar, salt and 1 cup flour. Beat with a spoon or electric mixer until smooth. Gradually stir in 1-1/2 cups flour, keeping dough smooth. If dough is still moist, stir in 1 tablespoon flour at a time to make a soft dough. Cover and let rise in a warm place until doubled in bulk, about 1 hour. Grease a 10- to 12-cup Bundt pan; set aside. Punch down dough; turn out onto a lightly oiled surface. Roll and stretch dough to make an 18" x 12" rectangle. Dough will be soft. Spread with 1/4 cup soft butter to within 1/2 inch of edges. Sprinkle with 1/2 cup sugar, then with cinnamon. Starting with a 12-inch side, roll up jelly-roll fashion. Place in prepared Bundt pan, seam-side down. Use scissors to snip halfway through roll, making cuts 1 inch apart. Let rise until dough doubles in bulk and fills pan. Preheat oven to 350F (175C). Bake 30 to 40 minutes or until a skewer inserted through center of loaf comes out clean. Cool 5 minutes in pan. Invert onto a rack; remove pan. Cool 15 minutes, then drizzle with glaze. Serve warm or toasted. After mixing in flour, dough can be refrigerated overnight. In morning, shape dough as directed above. Makes 1 coffee ring.

Powdered-Sugar Glaze:
In a small bowl, combine powdered sugar and coffee or water; beat until smooth.

Shape Variations

Cinnamon Leaves: Divide raised dough in half. On a lightly oiled board, roll and stretch 1 piece of dough to make a 12" x 8" rectangle. Spread 2 tablespoons soft butter over top. Sprinkle with 1/4 cup sugar and 1/2 teaspoon ground cinnamon. Beginning on a long side, roll up tightly, jelly-roll fashion. Repeat with remaining dough. Cut rolls into 2-inch slices. Use a sharp knife to make 2 evenly spaced, parallel slashes almost all the way through each 2-inch slice. Place on prepared baking sheets, with slashes up, fanning or pulling apart slightly. Cover and let rise in a warm place until almost doubled in bulk, about 45 minutes. Bake in a 350F (175C) oven, 12 to 15 minutes or until golden brown. Top with Powdered-Sugar Glaze, if desired. Makes 18 rolls.

Cinnamon Ears: Prepare dough as for Cinnamon Leaves, above, rolling jelly-roll fashion. Cut dough into 2-inch slices. Using the side of your index finger or the handle of a wooden spoon, press on center top of each slice. Edges will turn up. Place on prepared baking sheets. Let rise until doubled in bulk, about 45 minutes. Bake and glaze as for Cinnamon Leaves. Makes 18 rolls.

How to Make Cinnamon Ears

1/On a lightly oiled board, roll and stretch dough to make an 18" x 12" rectangle.

2/Use your finger or the handle of a wooden spoon to press crosswise on center of each slice.

White Potato Bread

Potetbrød—Norway

This light-textured bread is excellent for sandwiches or toasting.

1 (1/4-oz.) envelope active dry yeast
1/2 cup warm water or water potatoes
   were cooked in (110F, 45C)
1/4 cup sugar
1/2 cup butter, room temperature
3 eggs

2 teaspoons salt
1 cup cooked, mashed potatoes
   (may be leftover)
1 cup milk, scalded, cooled
6 to 7 cups all-purpose or bread flour

In a large bowl, stir yeast into warm water or potato water; let stand 5 minutes to soften. Add sugar, butter, eggs, salt, potatoes and milk; beat until smooth. Adding 1 cup at a time, beat in enough flour to make a stiff dough. Turn out onto a lightly floured board. Cover with a dry cloth; let stand 5 to 15 minutes. Wash and grease bowl; set aside. Grease two 9" x 5" loaf pans; set aside. Adding flour as necessary, knead dough until smooth, about 10 minutes. Place in greased bowl, turning to grease all sides. Cover and let rise in a warm place until doubled in bulk, about 2 hours. Punch down dough; divide in half. Shape each half into a loaf. Place in prepared pans; let rise in a warm place until doubled in bulk, 45 to 60 minutes. Preheat oven to 375F (190C). Bake 30 to 35 minutes or until loaves are golden brown and sound hollow when tapped with your fingers. Turn out of pans; cool on a rack. Makes 2 loaves.

Holiday Bread

Julekage—Denmark

A favorite in Denmark and Norway.

2 (1/4-oz.) envelopes active dry yeast
1/4 cup warm water (110F, 45C)
1/2 cup granulated sugar
2 cups milk, scalded, cooled
2 eggs, slightly beaten
1/2 cup butter, melted
2 teaspoons salt
1 teaspoon crushed cardamom seeds,
   if desired

6-1/2 to 7-1/2 cups all-purpose
   or bread flour
1 cup mixed, diced candied fruits, if desired
1 cup golden raisins
1 cup slivered blanched almonds, if desired
Egg Glaze, below
1/4 cup pearl sugar, page 8, or coarsely
   crushed sugar cubes, if desired
Almond Icing, page 140

In a large bowl, combine yeast, warm water and 1 tablespoon granulated sugar; let stand 5 minutes to soften. Stir in remaining granulated sugar, milk, eggs, butter, salt and cardamom, if desired. Add 3 cups flour; beat until smooth. Stir in enough of remaining flour to make a stiff dough. Turn out onto a lightly floured board. Cover with a dry cloth; let stand 8 to 10 minutes. Wash and grease bowl; set aside. Grease 3 round 8- or 9-inch cake pans; set aside. If desired, knead fruits and nuts into dough, adding flour as needed to prevent dough from being sticky. Knead about 10 minutes. Place dough in greased bowl, turning to grease all sides. Cover and let rise in a warm place until doubled in bulk, about 1-1/2 hours. Turn out dough onto a lightly oiled surface; divide dough into thirds. Shape each third into a round loaf; place, seam-side down, in prepared pans. Prepare Egg Glaze. Brush loaves with glaze. Let rise in a warm place until doubled in bulk, about 1 hour. Preheat oven to 375F (190C). Again brush loaves with glaze; sprinkle with pearl sugar or crushed sugar cubes, if desired. Bake 25 to 30 minutes or until golden brown and loaves sound hollow when tapped with your fingers. Turn out of pans; cool on a rack. Prepare Almond Icing. Spread over cooled loaves. Makes 3 loaves.

Egg Glaze for Breads & Lefse

In a small bowl, beat together, 1 egg, 1 teaspoon salt and 2 tablespoons milk. Brush glaze over yeast loaves after they have risen and before they are baked. If desired, brush over loaves again, 10 minutes before loaves are taken from the oven. To use with lefse, see Mrs. Olson's Flour Lefse, page 124.

To remove cardamom seeds from pods quickly, place the whole pods in a mortar or between two sheets of waxed paper. Crush the white pods with a pestle or hammer. Lift out the crushed pods and carefully blow onto the seeds to remove any remaining pod pieces. The dark seeds will remain.

Cardamom Coffee Braid

Pulla—Finland

Throughout Scandinavia, this bread is made into a variety of shapes for Christmas.

2 (1/4-oz.) envelopes active dry yeast
1/2 cup warm water (110F, 45C)
2 cups milk, scalded, cooled
1 cup granulated sugar
2 teaspoons salt
1 teaspoon freshly crushed cardamom
4 eggs, slightly beaten

8 to 9 cups all-purpose or bread flour
1/2 cup butter, melted
Egg Glaze, opposite
1/2 cup sliced almonds
1/2 cup pearl sugar, page 8, or
   coarsely crushed sugar cubes

In a large bowl, stir yeast into warm water; let stand 5 minutes to soften. Stir in milk, granulated sugar, salt, cardamom, eggs and 4 cups flour. Beat until smooth. Stir in butter until blended. Gradually stir in enough remaining flour to make a stiff dough. Turn out on a lightly floured board. Cover with a dry cloth; let stand 5 to 15 minutes. Wash and grease bowl; set aside. Grease 3 large baking sheets; set aside. Adding flour as needed, knead dough until smooth, about 10 minutes. Place dough in bowl, turning to grease all sides. Cover and let rise in a warm place until doubled in bulk, 1-1/2 to 2 hours. Punch down dough; let rise again until doubled in bulk, about 45 minutes. Turn out dough onto a lightly oiled surface. Divide into 3 portions. Working with one-third at a time, divide 1 portion of dough into 3 equal pieces. Roll each piece between palms of your hands and oiled surface to make 3 ropes, 30 inches long. Braid 3 ropes to make a loaf. Pinch ends together and tuck ends under loaf. Repeat with remaining dough. Place 1 braided loaf on each prepared baking sheet. Let rise until doubled in bulk, 45 to 60 minutes. Preheat oven to 375F (190C). Brush loaves with Egg Glaze; sprinkle with sliced almonds and pearl sugar or crushed sugar cubes. Bake 25 to 30 minutes or until crust is lightly browned and tender, not crisp; do not overbake. Cool on racks. Makes 3 braids.

Norwegian Rye Bread

Siktebrød—Norway

Thinly slice and use for Cream-Cheese & Salmon Smørrebrød, page 18.

1 (1/4-oz.) envelope active dry yeast
1/2 cup warm water (110F, 45C)
2 cups stirred rye flour
3/4 cup dark molasses

1/3 cup butter
1 teaspoon salt
2 cups boiling water
4-1/2 to 5 cups all-purpose or bread flour

In a small bowl, stir yeast into 1/2 cup warm water; let stand 5 minutes to soften. In large bowl of electric mixer, combine rye flour, molasses, butter and salt. Add boiling water; beat 2 minutes on medium speed. Cool slightly. Stir in yeast mixture. Adding 1 cup at a time, beat in enough all-purpose or bread flour to make a stiff dough. Turn out onto a lightly floured board. Cover with a dry cloth; let stand 5 to 15 minutes. Wash and grease bowl; set aside. Grease two 9" x 5" loaf pans; set aside. Adding flour as necessary, knead dough until smooth, about 10 minutes. Place in greased bowl, turning to grease all sides. Cover and let rise in a warm place until doubled in bulk, about 2 hours. Punch down dough; divide in half. Shape each half into a loaf. Place in prepared pans; let rise in a warm place until doubled in bulk, 45 to 60 minutes. Preheat oven to 350F (175C). Bake 35 to 45 minutes or until loaves are golden brown and sound hollow when tapped with your fingers. Turn out of pans; cool on a rack. Makes 2 loaves.

Rye Dipping Bread   Photo on pages 46-47.

Doppbröd—Sweden

On Christmas Eve, Swedes dip this bread into the Christmas-ham broth.

1 (1/4-oz.) envelope active dry yeast
1/4 cup warm water (110F, 45C)
1 tablespoon fennel seeds
1 tablespoon anise seeds
1 teaspoon salt
2 tablespoons sugar

2 tablespoons butter, melted
2 cups milk, scalded, cooled
3 cups stirred rye flour
3 to 3-1/2 cups all-purpose
   or bread flour

In a large bowl, stir yeast into warm water; let stand 5 minutes to soften. Crush fennel and anise seeds in a mortar and pestle, or pour into a plastic bag and pound with a hammer. Stir crushed seeds, salt, sugar, butter, milk and rye flour into yeast mixture; beat well. Adding 1 cup at a time, beat in enough all-purpose or bread flour to make a stiff dough. Turn out onto a lightly floured board. Cover with a dry cloth; let stand 5 to 15 minutes. Wash and grease bowl; set aside. Grease 2 large baking sheets; set aside. Adding flour as necessary, knead dough until smooth, about 10 minutes. Place in greased bowl, turning to grease all sides. Cover and let rise in a warm place until doubled in bulk, about 2 hours. Punch down dough; divide into 4 equal parts. Shape each into a round ball. Place 2 balls of dough on each prepared baking sheet. Let rise in a warm place until doubled in bulk, 45 to 60 minutes. Preheat oven to 375F (190C). Bake 25 minutes or until loaves sound hollow when tapped with your fingers. Cool on a rack. Makes 4 loaves.

Rye-Meal Bread

Ruisleipä—Finland

A sourdough version of this bread is popular in Finland and Sweden.

1 (1/4-oz.) envelope active dry yeast
2 teaspoons sugar
1-1/4 cups warm water (110F, 45C)
1-1/2 teaspoons salt

2 teaspoons shortening, melted
1-1/2 cups rye meal or whole-wheat flour
1-3/4 to 2 cups all-purpose or bread flour
1 tablespoon butter, melted

In a large bowl, stir yeast and sugar into warm water; let stand 5 minutes to soften. Stir in salt and shortening. Add rye meal or whole-wheat flour; beat until smooth. Adding 1 cup at a time, beat in enough all-purpose or bread flour to make a stiff dough. Turn out onto a lightly floured board. Cover with a dry cloth; let stand 5 to 15 minutes. Wash and grease bowl; set aside. Grease a large baking sheet; set aside. Adding flour as necessary to prevent sticking, knead dough until smooth, about 10 minutes. Place in greased bowl, turning to grease all sides. Cover and let rise in a warm place until doubled in bulk, about 2 hours. Punch down dough; shape into a ball. Flatten to a round loaf, 10 inches in diameter. Pressing with your fingers and thumbs, make a hole in center. Stretch until hole is 2 inches in diameter. Place shaped loaf on prepared baking sheet. Cover and let dough rise until doubled in bulk, about 1 hour. Preheat oven to 375F (190C). Use tines of a fork to make punctures over top of loaf. Bake 30 to 35 minutes or until golden brown. Brush top of hot loaf with butter. Cool on a rack. To serve, cut loaf into wedges. Split wedges horizontally. Makes 1 large loaf.

Danish Pumpernickel

Rugbrød—Denmark

This bread is close-textured, grainy and full of hearty flavor.

2 (1/4-oz.) envelopes active dry yeast
1-1/2 cups warm water (110F, 45C)
1/2 cup dark molasses
3 tablespoons butter, melted

2 tablespoons caraway seeds
1 teaspoon salt
2 cups rye meal or cracked wheat
3 to 4 cups all-purpose or bread flour

In a large bowl, stir yeast into warm water; let stand 5 minutes to soften. Stir in molasses, butter, caraway seeds and salt. Stir in rye meal or cracked wheat. Let stand 10 minutes. Adding 1 cup at a time, beat in enough flour to make a stiff dough. Turn out onto a lightly floured board. Cover with a dry cloth; let stand 5 to 15 minutes. Wash and grease bowl; set aside. Grease two 9" x 5" loaf pans; set aside. Adding flour as necessary, knead dough until smooth, about 10 minutes. Place in greased bowl, turning to grease all sides. Cover and let rise in a warm place until doubled in bulk, about 2 hours. Punch down dough; divide in half. Shape each half into a loaf. Place loaves, seam-side down, in prepared pans. Cover and let rise until doubled in bulk, about 1 hour. Preheat oven to 350F (175C). Brush tops of loaves with water, then bake 40 to 45 minutes or until loaves sound hollow when tapped with your fingers. Turn out of pans; cool on a rack. Makes 2 loaves.

Swedish Limpa   Photos on pages 69, 110-111.

Limpa—Sweden

The blended flavors of orange and anise makes this rye bread different and special.

1 (1/4-oz.) envelope active dry yeast
1/4 cup warm water (110F, 45C)
2 cups milk, scalded, cooled
1/2 cup dark molasses
1/2 cup vegetable oil
1/2 cup packed brown sugar
1-1/2 teaspoons salt

1-1/2 teaspoons caraway seeds
1-1/2 teaspoons fennel seeds
1-1/2 teaspoons anise seeds
Grated peel of 1 orange
1-1/2 cups stirred rye flour
5 to 6 cups all-purpose or bread flour

In a large bowl, stir yeast into warm water; let stand 5 minutes to soften. Stir in milk, molasses, oil, brown sugar and salt. Crush caraway seeds, fennel seeds and anise seeds in a mortar and pestle, or pour into a plastic bag and pound with a hammer. Add crushed seeds, orange peel and rye flour to yeast mixture. Beat until smooth. Adding 1 cup at a time, beat in enough all-purpose or bread flour to make a stiff dough. Turn out onto a lightly floured board. Cover with a dry cloth; let stand 5 to 15 minutes. Wash and grease bowl; set aside. Grease 2 round 8- or 9-inch cake pans; set aside. Adding flour as necessary, knead dough until smooth, about 10 minutes. Place in greased bowl, turning to grease all sides. Cover and let rise in a warm place until doubled in bulk, 1 to 1-1/2 hours. Punch down dough; divide in half. Shape each half into a round loaf. Place loaves, seam-side down, in prepared pans. Cover and let rise until doubled in bulk, about 1 hour. Preheat oven to 375F (190C). Bake 35 minutes or until loaves sound hollow when tapped with your fingers. Turn out of pans; cool on a rack. Makes 2 loaves.

Whole-Wheat Bread

Hvetekake—Norway

Norwegians prefer whole-grain breads such as this for sandwiches.

1 (1/4-oz.) envelope active dry yeast	1/2 cup water
2 cups warm water (110F, 45C)	3 tablespoons butter, melted
2 tablespoons granulated sugar	2 teaspoons salt
3 cups all-purpose or bread flour	3 to 3-1/2 cups whole-wheat flour
1/2 cup packed brown sugar	Water

In a large bowl, stir yeast into 2 cups warm water; let stand 5 minutes to soften. Stir in granulated sugar and all-purpose or bread flour. Beat until smooth. Cover and let rise in a warm place, 30 minutes or until bubbles begin to form. In a small bowl, stir brown sugar into 1/2 cup water until dissolved. Stir in butter and salt. Stir brown-sugar mixture into yeast mixture. Gradually stir in enough whole-wheat flour to make a stiff dough. Lightly sprinkle a board with whole-wheat flour. Turn out dough onto floured board. Cover with a dry cloth; let stand 5 to 15 minutes. Wash and grease bowl; set aside. Grease 2 round 8- or 9-inch cake pans, 9" x 5" loaf pans or large baking sheets; set aside. Adding flour as necessary, knead dough until smooth, about 10 minutes. Place in greased bowl, turning to grease all sides. Cover and let rise in a warm place until doubled in bulk, 1-1/2 to 2 hours. Punch down dough; divide in half. Shape each half into a round, oblong or French-bread shape. Place shaped loaves in pans or on baking sheets. Cover and let rise until doubled in bulk, about 1 hour. Preheat oven to 350F (175C). Brush tops of raised loaves with water. Bake 40 to 45 minutes or until loaves sound hollow when tapped with your fingers. Turn out of pans; cool on racks. Makes 2 loaves.

Country Oat Loaf Photos on pages 33 and opposite.

Havremelsbrød—Denmark

Rolled-oats topping was a special touch from a Danish farmwoman.

2 cups milk, boiling	1 (1/4-oz.) envelope active dry yeast
1 cup uncooked rolled oats	1/4 cup warm water (110F, 45C)
2 tablespoons butter	5 to 5-1/2 cups all-purpose or bread flour
1/4 cup dark molasses	Egg Glaze, page 132
1 teaspoon salt	Rolled oats

In a large bowl, pour boiling milk over 1 cup rolled oats. Stir in butter, molasses and salt; let stand 30 minutes. In a small bowl, stir yeast into warm water; let soften 5 minutes. Stir into oats mixture. Adding 1 cup at a time, beat in enough flour to make a stiff dough. Turn out onto a lightly floured board. Cover with a dry cloth; let stand 5 to 15 minutes. Wash and grease bowl; set aside. Grease 2 round 9-inch cake pans; set aside. Adding flour as necessary, knead dough until smooth, about 10 minutes. Place in greased bowl, turning to grease all sides. Cover and let rise in a warm place until doubled in bulk, about 2 hours. Punch down dough; divide in half. Shape each half into a round loaf. Place loaves, seam-side down, in prepared pans. Cover and let rise until doubled in bulk, about 1 hour. Brush loaves with Egg Glaze, then sprinkle heavily with uncooked rolled oats. Preheat oven to 375F (190C). Bake 35 to 45 minutes or until loaves sound hollow when tapped with your fingers. Turn out of pans; cool on a rack. Makes 2 loaves.

Clockwise from top: St. Lucia Cats, page 127; Cardamom Coffee Braid, page 133; Country Oat Loaf. At bottom left: Pearl Sugar.

DANISH PASTRY

Window shopping in Denmark can send a pastry addict into euphoria! Shelves in the windows of every baker's shop are filled with variation upon variation of treats made with sweet, flaky, yeast-risen Danish-Pastry Dough. Danes call it *Vienna Bread* or *Wienerbrød*. Germans and Austrians call it *Copenhagen Pastry*.

Danish pastry is made by repeatedly rolling and folding lightly sweetened, cardamom-flavored yeast dough and butter. This produces layer upon layer of thin, buttery, crisp pastry. As you prepare the pastry, keep the dough cold. Be sure to include the chilling steps between each rolling and folding step. Chilled dough is easier to handle, and during the chilling, you can relax. A marble rolling pin will hold the cold and because of its weight, make your job of rolling easier.

For perfect Danish pastry, use the best grade of butter you can purchase. Unsalted, Grade-AA butter gives the finest results, but lightly salted butter can be used. Rolled butter, that comes in one-pound blocks and is wrapped in a single piece of paper, is a lower-grade butter. It has more liquid incorporated with the fat. It will not make good Danish pastry.

The recipe for Danish-Pastry Dough is used in all but one of the following variations. When only half of the dough is used, wrap the remaining dough in plastic wrap and store it in the refrigerator. Use it within four to five days.

Bear Claws   Photo on page 143.

Wienerbrøds Kamme — Denmark

The literal translation is "Danish-pastry combs."

1 recipe Danish-Pastry Dough, page 140
1 recipe Vanilla Buttercream, below
1 recipe Almond Buttercream, page 142
Water

1 cup pearl sugar, page 8, or
  coarsely crushed sugar cubes
1 cup sliced almonds
1 recipe Almond Icing, page 140, if desired

Divide pastry into 4 equal pieces. On a lightly floured board, roll 1 piece into a 12-inch square. Spread one-fourth of Vanilla Buttercream down center third of pastry; top with one-fourth of Almond Buttercream. Fold right and left thirds over center. Pinch edges of pastry to seal. Lightly roll crosswise with a rolling pin until pastry is 5 to 6 inches wide. Cut dough crosswise into 2-inch slices. On long side of each 2-inch slice, cut 4 parallel slashes, equidistant apart, to within 1/2 inch of other edge. Repeat with remaining dough. Pour water 2 inches deep into a medium bowl. Combine sugar and almonds in another medium bowl. Quickly dip top side of each bear claw in and out of water, then into sugar mixture. Arrange on an ungreased baking sheet, coated-side up, curving slightly to open claws. Cover with plastic wrap; let rise 45 minutes. Preheat oven to 400F (205C). Remove plastic wrap. Bake 13 to 15 minutes or until golden brown. Cool on a rack. Drizzle with Almond Icing, if desired. Makes 24 bear claws.

Snails   Photo on page 143.

Snegle — Denmark

These are similar to cinnamon rolls.

1 recipe Danish-Pastry Dough, page 140
1/2 recipe Vanilla Buttercream, below
1 recipe Almond Buttercream, page 142

1 egg, beaten
1 recipe Coffee Glaze, page 144

Divide pastry in half; refrigerate 1 piece. On a lightly floured board, roll remaining half into a 16" x 8" rectangle. Spread with half of Vanilla Buttercream. Top with half of Almond Buttercream. Starting on a long side, roll up jelly-roll fashion. Cut roll crosswise into 16 slices. Place each slice in a paper muffin-cup liner. Arrange filled liners on an ungreased baking sheet. Repeat with remaining dough. Cover and let rise in a warm place, 45 minutes. Preheat oven to 400F (205C). Brush pastries with beaten egg. Bake 12 to 15 minutes or until lightly browned. Brush hot baked pastries with Coffee Glaze. Makes 32 snails.

Vanilla Buttercream

Vanille Smørcreme — Denmark

Use this sweet mixture as a filling and an icing for Danish pastry.

1/2 cup butter, room temperature
1 cup powdered sugar

1/2 teaspoon vanilla extract

Blend butter into powdered sugar. Blend in vanilla. Makes about 1 cup.

Danish-Pastry Dough

Weinerbrød—Denmark

This flaky yeast pastry is known as "Copenhagen dough" in Germany and Austria.

1-1/4 cups unsalted grade AA butter,
  chilled
2 (1/4-oz.) envelopes active dry yeast
1/4 cup warm water (110F, 45C)
1/2 cup evaporated milk, room temperature
2 eggs, room temperature

1/2 teaspoon crushed cardamom seeds,
  if desired
1 teaspoon salt
1/4 cup sugar
2-1/2 to 3 cups all-purpose flour

Place butter between two 12-inch squares of plastic wrap. Pound with a rolling pin until butter can be shaped without breaking. Leaving butter between pieces of plastic wrap, roll to a 10" x 8" rectangle; refrigerate. Place a 36" x 24" breadboard in refrigerator or freezer to chill, or place 2 large baking sheets in freezer to chill. In a large bowl, stir yeast into warm water; let stand 5 minutes to soften. Stir in milk, eggs, cardamom if desired, salt and sugar until blended. Add 2-1/2 cups flour all at once. Beat until dough comes away from side of bowl. Add more flour as needed to make a stiff dough. Or, pour yeast mixture into a food processor fitted with metal blade. Add milk, eggs, cardamom if desired, salt and sugar; process until blended. Add 2-1/2 cups flour; process until dough comes away from side of bowl. Add more flour if needed. Dough will be soft, glossy and smooth. Grease a large bowl; place dough in bowl, turning to grease all sides. Cover with plastic wrap; refrigerate 30 minutes to let dough relax. Dust chilled breadboard with flour, or place chilled baking sheets on a board, 2 to 3 minutes, to chill board; dust chilled board with flour. **To roll dough:** Turn out dough onto floured board. Dust ball of dough with flour, then roll into an 18" x 12" rectangle. Remove plastic wrap from chilled butter. Place chilled butter crosswise on 1 end of pastry, about 1 inch from all 3 edges. Fold other half of dough over butter. Press out any air bubbles; pinch edges to seal. Roll out dough to make as large a square as possible, but at least 20 inches square. Puncture bubbles as they form; pinch dough to seal any holes that form. Fold pastry square in thirds, folding right and left thirds over center. Seal layers together by pressing with side of your hands, or lightly roll with a rolling pin. If necessary, dust board and dough lightly with flour to prevent sticking. Again, fold dough in thirds; press layers together. Wrap folded dough in plastic wrap; refrigerate 15 to 30 minutes to let dough relax and chill. Roll chilled dough to make a 24-inch square. Fold into thirds; press or roll lightly to seal layers. Again fold in thirds. Wrap in plastic wrap and refrigerate 15 to 30 minutes. For a third time, repeat rolling, folding and chilling. During final chilling, prepare for 1 of following pastries. Wrapped dough may be stored in refrigerator 4 to 5 days. Makes about 1-1/2 pounds dough.

Almond Icing

Mandelglasur—Denmark

Use this smooth icing on Danish pastry, cookies and cupcakes.

1 cup powdered sugar
2 tablespoons water

1 teaspoon vegetable oil
1/2 teaspoon almond extract

In a small bowl, blend powdered sugar with water, oil and almond extract until smooth. Add more water if necessary to make an icing thin enough to drizzle. Makes about 1/2 cup.

How to Make Danish Pastry

1/Roll butter into a flat slab. Place chilled butter crosswise on 1 end of pastry. Fold dough over butter.

2/Press out any air bubbles. Pinch edges to seal in butter. Fold and roll out three times.

3/To shape finished dough for Bear Claws, spread buttercreams over center third. Fold dough over.

4/Cut dough into 2-inch slices. Cut 4 crosswise parallel slashes to within 1/2 inch of edge. Decorate.

Marzipan Kringle

Kringle—Denmark

So crisp, light and rich, you can serve this as a birthday cake for a Danish-pastry addict!

1 (1/4-oz.) envelope active dry yeast
1/2 cup warm milk (110F, 45C)
1 tablespoon sugar
3 egg yolks, slightly beaten
1 cup whipping cream
3-1/2 cups all-purpose flour
1/4 cup sugar
1 teaspoon salt

1/2 cup butter, chilled
Marzipan Filling, see below
1/4 cup pearl sugar, page 8,
    coarsely crushed sugar cubes or
    granulated sugar
1 egg white, slightly beaten
1/4 cup sliced almonds

Marzipan Filling:
1 (8-oz.) pkg. almond paste
1/2 cup chopped almonds
1/2 cup sugar

1 egg white
1 teaspoon ground cinnamon
1 teaspoon almond extract

In a medium bowl, combine yeast, milk, 1 tablespoon sugar, egg yolks and cream; let stand 10 minutes. In a large bowl, blend flour, 1/4 cup sugar and salt. Cut in butter until pieces are size of kidney beans. Add yeast mixture; fold in only until dry ingredients are moistened. Cover with plastic wrap; refrigerate 12 to 24 hours. Prepare Marzipan Filling. Turn out dough onto a lightly floured board; dust dough with flour. Using a rolling pin, pound dough until smooth and 3/4 inch thick. Roll dough to a 24-inch square. If necessary, fold in half, then knead 4 or 5 times to make dough easier to roll. Spread filling to within 1 inch of edges. Roll up tightly, jelly-roll fashion. Sprinkle work surface with pearl sugar, crushed sugar cubes or granulated sugar. Roll dough in sugar. Brush surface of dough with egg white, then roll in sugar again. Generously grease a large baking sheet. Shape into a large pretzel by laying rolled dough on prepared baking sheet, curved like a *U,* with ends even. About 5 inches from ends, loop sides of *U* around each other. Tuck ends under closed part of *U.* Again brush with egg white; sprinkle with almonds. Cover and let rise in a warm place, 40 minutes. Kringle will not double in bulk. Preheat oven to 375F (190C). Bake 25 to 30 minutes or until golden brown. Makes 1 large kringle or 12 servings.

Marzipan Filling:
Break almond paste into small pieces. In a medium bowl, combine almond-paste pieces and remaining ingredients. Press with back of a wooden spoon until blended.

Almond Buttercream

Mandel Smørcreme—Denmark

Almond is a favorite filling flavor for Danish pastry.

1/4 cup almond paste
1/4 cup butter

1/2 cup powdered sugar

In a medium bowl or in food processor fitted with metal blade, blend almond paste, butter and powdered sugar until smooth. Makes about 3/4 cup.

Top to bottom: Snails, Bear Claws, both page 139; Marzipan Kringle.

Boston Cake

Smørkage—Denmark

In Finland and Sweden this is known as "Bostonkakku."

1 recipe Danish-Pastry Dough, page 140
1/3 cup sugar
2 tablespoons ground cinnamon

1 recipe Vanilla Buttercream, page 139
1 recipe Coffee Glaze, below

Roll out pastry to as large a rectangle as your work surface will allow, preferably 36'' x 20'', but at least a 20-inch square. If pastry is hard to roll, let it rest 30 seconds, then continue rolling. In a small bowl, blend sugar and cinnamon. Spread dough with Vanilla Buttercream to within 1 inch of edges, then sprinkle with sugar-cinnamon mixture. Beginning on a long side, roll up jelly-roll fashion. Cut roll into 8 equal pieces. Generously butter a 2-1/2- to 3-quart ring mold or tube pan. Place dough cut-side down in pan, spacing evenly to allow for rising. Cover and let rise 1-1/2 to 2 hours or until pastry is light and puffy. Preheat oven to 350F (175C). Bake 45 to 55 minutes or until golden brown and a skewer inserted 2-1/2 inches from center comes out clean. Cool on a rack 5 minutes, then turn out of pan. Drizzle with Coffee Glaze. Makes about 24 servings.

Danish-Pastry Braid

Wienerfletning—Denmark

Folding the dough makes this look like a braid—although it isn't one.

1/2 recipe Danish-Pastry Dough, page 140
1/2 recipe Vanilla Buttercream, page 139
1/2 recipe Almond Buttercream, page 142

1 egg, slightly beaten
1 recipe Almond Icing, page 140
Toasted sliced almonds

On a lightly floured surface, roll out pastry to a 24'' x 8'' rectangle. Cut in half, making two 12'' x 8'' pieces. Place each on a separate ungreased baking sheet. Spread half of Vanilla Buttercream lengthwise down center third of each pastry; top with half of Almond Buttercream. With a sharp knife, make slashes at a 45-degree angle from buttercream mixture to outer edges of pastry, at 1-inch intervals. Alternately fold strips over filling in a criss-cross fashion, to give pastry a braided appearance. Cover and let rise 1 hour at room temperature. Preheat oven to 400F (205C). Brush with beaten egg. Bake 13 to 15 minutes or until golden brown and crisp. While still warm, decorate with Almond Icing and almonds. Makes 12 servings.

Coffee Glaze

Kaffeglasur—Denmark

Use this glaze on Danish pastry, cinnamon rolls or Kaffekrans, page 130.

1 cup powdered sugar
2 tablespoons hot strong coffee, or
   1 teaspoon instant coffee dissolved in
   2 tablespoons hot water

2 tablespoons butter, room temperature

In a small bowl, blend powdered sugar, coffee and butter until smooth. Makes about 1/2 cup.

COFFEETABLE CELEBRATIONS

In Scandinavia, the term "coffeetable" refers to a three-course refreshment table. Coffeetables are appropriate for an open house, wedding, engagement, birthday, nameday, confirmation or baptism, anniversary, Christmas, St. Lucia Day or in honor of a visiting dignitary. Coffeetables are offered in public places too, such as at the opening of a new business, after a public meeting or the performance of an artist. Coffeetables are served at any time of day or night.

If you are served a coffeetable in Finland at Christmastime, you will have seven courses of baked goods and sip at least four cups of coffee.

The most formal coffeetable must include at least seven items. There are three courses: bread with cheese or open-face sandwiches; uniced cake such as pound cake; and a fruit- or cream-filled cake or torte. At least four varieties of cookies complete the menu. You are always served several cups of richly brewed coffee in cups slightly larger than demitasse cups. For large groups, cof-

feetables are reduced to a simpler menu—bread, cookies and perhaps some small tarts.

The breads served will vary, depending on where you are in Scandinavia. Open-face sandwiches are common in Denmark. In Norway, *lefse,* a pliable, flat, potato bread, often appears on the coffeetable. In Finland, *pulla,* a cardamom-flavored braid, is always present.

When serving yourself, begin with the least sweet of the items offered. With the first cup of coffee, select a piece of bread with a thin slice of cheese or a sandwich. With the second cup of coffee, take the uniced cake. With the third cup of coffee, help yourself to the filled cake or torte.

During the holiday season, sweet breads, cakes, cookies and pastries are served. For Christmas, *Glögg,* a hot, spiced-wine punch may be served as a substitute for coffee.

In the following menu, prepare one item from each of the first three courses and make four different cookies.

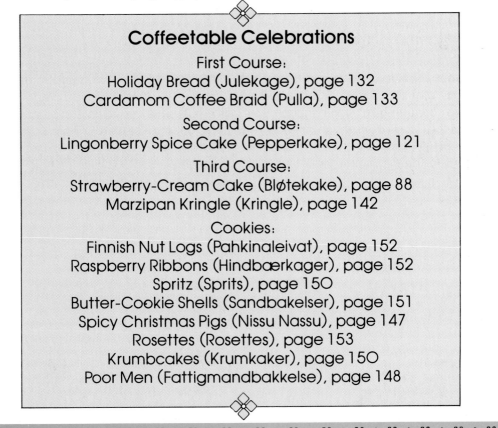

Coffeetable Celebrations

First Course:
Holiday Bread (Julekage), page 132
Cardamom Coffee Braid (Pulla), page 133

Second Course:
Lingonberry Spice Cake (Pepperkake), page 121

Third Course:
Strawberry-Cream Cake (Bløtekake), page 88
Marzipan Kringle (Kringle), page 142

Cookies:
Finnish Nut Logs (Pahkinaleivat), page 152
Raspberry Ribbons (Hindbærkager), page 152
Spritz (Sprits), page 150
Butter-Cookie Shells (Sandbakelser), page 151
Spicy Christmas Pigs (Nissu Nassu), page 147
Rosettes (Rosettes), page 153
Krumbcakes (Krumkaker), page 150
Poor Men (Fattigmandbakkelse), page 148

SCANDINAVIAN COOKIES

Cookies! Cookies! Cookies! A self-respecting Scandinavian baker will not lay down her wooden spoon until she has baked at least a dozen varieties for Christmas! But that is not the only time she bakes cookies. Scandinavians enjoy informal entertaining, and are always ready for the unexpected visitor.

Several years ago we visited a farm family who stored butter cookies in the cool depths of their well during the summertime. Today, most families keep a supply of cookies in the freezer. You can purchase a great variety of cookies and fancy little cakes at the confectioner's and in the market. However, they are expensive, so most homemakers prefer to make their own.

During the summer in Scandinavia, it is light day and night. Therefore, any time can be coffeetime—the time for getting together. A guest will never protest more than twice if asked to remove an overcoat and come in. The encounter might be as follows: "Please come in and have a cup of coffee." "Honestly, I couldn't." "But really, you must try a little piece!" "Well, just a little . . . ."

Butter cookies. are my favorites. With slight variations, they are common to all Scandinavian countries. In fact, it is difficult to distinguish between countries, because they cross borders. Because they are so similar, I've given you a basic dough and several variations.

By far the most popular cookie throughout the year is the ginger cookie or *pepperkaker*. There are various spellings of the same cookie throughout Scandinavia. Spicy Christmas Pigs are technically ginger cookies. These cookies appear in bakeries and food markets all over Finland, beginning with Advent. When children see these decorated, pig-shape cookies, they know the Christmas season has arrived. The symbolism of the pig probably dates back to when each family raised a pet pig for the holiday meals. The cookies are decorated by writing *Nissu* or *Nassu* on them, or they can be decorated with a child's name.

The same dough can be cut into other shapes. The Dala horse, from Dalarna, Sweden, is a classic Christmas-cookie shape. Or, a hostess may pipe the names of her dinner guests on heartshape ginger cookies and use them as place cards. Gingerbread men and ladies, Christmas trees, Santa Clauses and roosters are other classic shapes for these cookies.

Spicy Christmas Pigs   Photos on pages 46-47, 149.

Nissu Nassu—Finland

When children see these pig-shape cookies in Finnish bakeries, they know Christmas is coming!

2/3 cup butter, room temperature
3/4 cup packed brown sugar
1 tablespoon ground cinnamon
2 teaspoons ground ginger

1-1/2 teaspoons ground cloves
1-1/2 teaspoons baking soda
2-1/2 cups all-purpose flour
1/4 cup water

Royal Icing:
1 egg white
3 to 4 cups unsifted powdered sugar

1 to 2 tablespoons water

In a medium bowl or food processor fitted with metal blade, mix butter, brown sugar, cinnamon, ginger, cloves, baking soda, flour and water until blended and dough forms a smooth ball. If dough is very soft, refrigerate 30 minutes. Preheat oven to 375F (190C). Lightly grease a large baking sheet; set aside. On a lightly floured surface, roll dough 1/8 inch thick. Cut with a pig- or other animal-shape cookie cutter. Place cut-out cookies on prepared baking sheet. Bake 7 to 10 minutes or until crisp and lightly browned. Cool on a rack. Prepare Royal Icing. To decorate cookies, pipe on features of animals or other decorative designs. With icing, write *Nissu* on half of pig-shape cookies and *Nassu* on other half. Or, write family names or names of guests. Use as place-cards, if desired. Makes 60 to 70 cookies.

Royal Icing:
In a medium bowl, beat egg white until frothy; gradually beat in powdered sugar, making an icing thin enough to drizzle. Or, spoon icing into pastry bag fitted with a thin writing tip. Press icing out to write names.

Vanilla Wreaths   Photo on page 23.

Vanillekranser—Denmark

These delicate, buttery cookie rings are traditionally served at Christmas.

2 cups all-purpose flour
1 cup sugar
1/8 teaspoon baking powder
Pinch salt

1 cup butter, room temperature
1 egg, slightly beaten
1/2 cup blanched almonds, ground
1 teaspoon vanilla extract

Lightly grease a large baking sheet, or line with parchment paper; set aside. Preheat oven to 375F (190C). In a large bowl, combine flour, sugar, baking powder and salt; blend. Stir in butter with a fork until mixture is crumbly. Add egg, almonds and vanilla; blend until dough is smooth and pliable. Refrigerate 30 minutes. Spoon dough into a cookie press. Attach 1/4-inch tube tip. Press dough through tube onto a lightly floured board, making long strips. Cut in 5-inch lengths. Working with 1 piece at a time, place on prepared baking sheet, overlapping ends to make small circles. Do not pinch ends together. Bake in preheated oven 8 minutes or until lightly browned. Cool on a rack. Makes about 96 cookies.

Gingerbread Cookies

Pepperkaker — Norway

These cookies are popular all year in Scandinavia, but are always present at Christmastime.

2/3 cup butter, room temperature
3/4 cup packed light-brown sugar
3 to 4 tablespoons water
2 tablespoons dark molasses
2 cups all-purpose flour
1 tablespoon ground cinnamon

1-1/2 teaspoons ground cloves
1 teaspoon ground ginger
1 teaspoon ground cardamom
1 teaspoon grated lemon peel
1 teaspoon baking soda

In large bowl of electric mixer, cream butter and brown sugar until blended. Beat in 3 tablespoons water and molasses until smooth. In a medium bowl, combine flour, cinnamon, cloves, ginger, cardamom, lemon peel and baking soda. Gradually stir into molasses mixture to make a stiff dough. Add remaining 1 tablespoon water, if necessary, to shape dough into a ball. Wrap ball of dough in plastic wrap. Refrigerate 30 minutes. Preheat oven to 350F (175C). Line baking sheets with parchment paper, or grease lightly. On a lightly floured surface, roll dough 1/8 to 1/4 inch thick. Cut into hearts, gingerbread men and ladies or other shapes. Arrange on prepared baking sheets. Bake 10 to 12 minutes or until firm but not browned. Cool on a rack. Makes about 48 cookies.

Poor Men

Fattigmandbakkelse — Norway

Delicate, crisp, diamond-shaped delicacies.

2 eggs
2 tablespoons whipping cream
1 teaspoon vanilla extract
3 tablespoons granulated sugar

1-1/2 cups all-purpose flour
Fat for deep-frying
Powdered sugar

In a large bowl, beat eggs, cream and vanilla until blended. Stir in granulated sugar and flour, making a stiff dough. On a lightly floured board, roll out half of dough, 1/8 inch thick. Cut dough in 1-inch strips; cut stips, diagonally, into 2-1/2 inches pieces. Make a slit 1-inch long down center on the diagonal between 2 corners farthest apart. Pull 1 end through slit to make a twist out of the dough. Pour oil 2 inches deep into a medium saucepan. Place over medium heat. Heat to 375F (190C). Use a slotted spoon to lower twisted dough carefully into hot fat. Cook about 2 minutes or until golden brown on both sides. Drain on paper towels. When cool, dust with powdered sugar. To serve, arrange on a tray. To store, pack in a container with a tight-fitting lid; store in freezer. Makes 48 cookies.

Browning of baked goods is more even and cleanup is easier when you cover baking sheets with parchment paper rather than greasing them.

Top row: Gingerbread Cookies, Spicy Christmas Pigs, page 147; center: Poor Men; bottom: Raspberry Ribbons, page 152.

Butter-Cookie Dough

Pikkuleipienperustaikina—Finland

This basic dough can be shaped many ways to prepare Scandinavian holiday cookies.

1 cup butter, room temperature
1/2 cup sugar
1 egg, slightly beaten
2-1/2 cups all-purpose flour

1 teaspoon vanilla extract
1/4 teaspoon salt
1 to 2 teaspoons water, if needed

In a medium bowl, or food processor fitted with the metal blade, mix butter, sugar, egg, flour, vanilla and salt until a smooth, pliable cookie dough forms. If mixture seems dry, work in 1 to 2 teaspoons water. Gather dough into a ball; knead slightly. Wrap in plastic wrap; refrigerate 30 minutes or until ready to use. Dough can be stored in refrigerator up to 1 week. Use dough in following recipes. Makes about 2 cups dough.

Krumbcakes   Photo on pages 46-47.

Krumkaker—Norway

These delicate, crisp cookies are a traditional Norwegian holiday treat.

1 cup sugar
2 eggs
1/2 cup butter, melted
2/3 cup milk

1-1/3 cups all-purpose flour
1 teaspoon crushed cardamom seeds
Water, if necessary

In a medium bowl, combine sugar, eggs and butter. Use a whisk to beat in milk until mixture is blended and smooth. Stir in flour until blended. Stir in cardamom. Preheat *krumkaker iron,* page 7, over medium heat until a drop of water sizzles when dropped on top. Open iron; lightly brush inside top and bottom with shortening, oil or melted butter. Spoon 1 tablespoon batter onto center of hot iron. Close iron. Bake about 1 minute on each side or until cookie is lightly browned. Insert tip of a knife under cookie to remove from iron; roll hot cookie into a cigar or cone shape. Cool on a rack. Cookies become crisp as they cool. Repeat with remaining batter. If batter becomes thick, stir in water, 1 tablespoon at a time. Store in airtight containers. These freeze well. Makes 25 to 30 krumbcakes.

Spritz

Sprits—Sweden

Popular all year, but especially during the holidays.

Butter-Cookie Dough, above
Colored sugar

Preheat oven to 350F (175C). Do not refrigerate cookie dough. Fill a cookie press with dough as manufacturer directs. Select plate and fit onto press. Press dough onto an ungreased baking sheet. Sprinkle with colored sugar. Bake 10 to 12 minutes or only until cookies are firm and lightly browned around edges. Do not overbake. Cool on a rack. Makes about 100 cookies.

Butter-Cookie Shells

Sandbakelser—Sweden

These look like they ought to have a filling, but they don't.

Butter-Cookie Dough, opposite
1/2 teaspoon almond extract

Preheat oven to 375F (190C). When preparing Butter-Cookie Dough, add 1/2 teaspoon almond extract with vanilla. Refrigerate dough 30 minutes. Divide into fourths. On a lightly floured surface, roll 1 piece of dough to a rectangle, 1/8 inch thick. Arrange 12 *sandbakelser tins,* page 8, close together. Carefully lift dough and place over tins, letting dough drape into tins. Roll a rolling pin across tops of tins to cut dough. Dip your fingers in flour, then press dough evenly into tins. Bake 12 to 15 minutes or until cookie shells are lightly browned. Cool on a rack. Serve open-side down. Makes 48 (2-inch) shells or 60 to 72 (1-1/2-inch) shells.

Variation
Spicy Sandbakkelser: Add 1/4 teaspoon ground cardamom to Butter-Cookie Dough.

How to Make Butter-Cookie Shells

1/Carefully lift dough and drape over sandbakelser tins. Roll rolling pin over tins to cut dough.

2/Carefully press dough into tins with your fingers. Do not stretch dough.

Finnish Nut Logs

Pähkinäleivät—Finland

These nut-crusted, golden cookies are a year-round favorite in Finland.

Butter-Cookie Dough, page 150
1 egg

1/4 cup finely chopped almonds
2 tablespoons sugar

Preheat oven to 350F (175C). Lightly grease a large baking sheet; set aside. Divide cookie dough into fourths. Rolling each between your hands and a lightly floured surface, shape into ropes, 1/2 inch thick. Cut crosswise in 2-inch slices. In a small shallow dish, beat egg until well blended and smooth. In another small bowl, combine almonds and sugar. Roll cookie slices or logs first in beaten egg, then in sugar mixture. Place 2 inches apart on prepared baking sheet. Bake 12 to 15 minutes or until lightly browned. Cool on a rack. Makes about 48 cookies.

Raspberry Ribbons   Photo on page 149.

Hindbærkager—Denmark

These jam-filled cookie ribbons are a quick way to add color to the cookie tray.

Butter-Cookie Dough, page 150
1/2 cup raspberry jam or jelly

1/2 cup powdered sugar
2 tablespoons milk

Preheat oven to 375F (190C). Divide cookie dough into fourths. Rolling each between your hands and a lightly floured surface, shape into ropes, about 1/2 inch thick. Place ropes on an ungreased baking sheet about 2 inches apart. With side of your little finger, press a long groove down length of each strand. Bake 10 minutes. Spoon jam or jelly into groove. Bake 5 to 10 minutes longer or until edges are lightly browned. In a small bowl, beat powdered sugar and milk to make a glaze. Brush or drizzle glaze over hot cookies. Cut logs diagonally into 1-inch slices. Makes about 96 cookies.

Almond Cookies

Mandelkaker—Norway

These nut-topped cookies are used on Coffeetables all year long.

Butter-Cookie Dough, page 150
1 teaspoon almond extract
36 pieces slivered almonds
18 candied cherries, halved

1/2 cup powdered sugar
2 tablespoons whipping cream or
** evaporated milk**

Preheat oven to 350F (175C). When preparing Butter-Cookie Dough, add 1 teaspoon almond extract with vanilla. Shape dough into 1-inch balls. Arrange on an ungreased baking sheet, 1 inch apart. Press a piece of almond or a halved cherry into center of each cookie. Bake 12 to 15 minutes, only until cookies are firm and begin to brown around edges. Cool on a rack. In a small bowl, blend powdered sugar and cream or evaporated milk to make a thin icing. Drizzle icing over nut or fruit on each cookie. Makes about 36 cookies.

Rosettes

Rosettes — Sweden

Rosette irons come with interchangeable shapes.

2 eggs
2 teaspoons granulated sugar
1/4 teaspoon salt
1 cup milk

1 cup all-purpose flour
Oil for deep-frying
Powdered sugar

In a small bowl, beat eggs, granulated sugar, salt and milk with a whisk until blended. Beat in flour to make a smooth batter. Let stand 30 minutes. Pour oil 2 inches deep into a medium saucepan. Over medium heat, heat to 375F (190C). Place rosette iron into hot oil for 1 minute; shake off excess oil. Immediately dip into batter, being careful not to let batter come over top edge of iron. Immerse batter-covered iron into hot fat. Shake iron to loosen batter while immersed in hot oil. Fry about 1 minute or until golden brown. Use a slotted spoon to lift cooked rosette from hot oil. Drain on paper towels. To serve, dust with powdered sugar. Makes about 36 rosettes.

Blueberry Bars   Photo on pages 110-111.

Mustikkapiirakka — Finland

Delightful combination — lemon-accented blueberry filling and butter crust.

Butter Crust, see below
2 cups fresh or frozen,
   unsweetened blueberries
1/4 cup sugar
1 tablespoon lemon juice

1 tablespoon grated lemon peel
2 tablespoons cornstarch
1/4 teaspoon salt
1 tablespoon sugar

Butter Crust:
2-1/2 cups all-purpose flour
1/2 teaspoon baking powder
1/2 cup sugar

1 cup butter, room temperature
1 egg, slightly beaten

Prepare Butter-Crust dough; refrigerate 30 minutes. In a medium saucepan, combine blueberries, 1/4 cup sugar, lemon juice, lemon peel, cornstarch and salt. Over low heat, stir until mixture is blended. Increase heat to medium. Stirring constantly, cook until thickened. Cool to room temperature. Preheat oven to 375F (190C). Butter a 13" x 9" baking pan; set aside. Divide chilled dough into three-fourths and one-fourth portions. On a lightly floured surface, roll out large portion to a 15" x 11" rectangle for bottom crust. Roll around rolling pin; unroll into prepared baking pan. Dough will cover bottom of pan and extend 1 inch up each side. Spoon cooled filling into pastry. Roll out reserved dough, 1/8-inch thick; cut into 1/2-inch strips. Criss-cross strips over blueberry filling to make a lattice top. Sprinkle with 1 tablespoon sugar. Bake 25 to 30 minutes or until lattice is golden brown. Cool to room temperature. To serve, cut in 3-inch squares. Makes 12 servings.

Butter Crust:
In a large bowl, combine flour, baking powder and sugar. Using an electric mixer or wooden spoon, blend in butter. Add egg and continue mixing until a pliable dough forms.

Chocolate-Dipped Orange Sticks

Orangesmåkager—Denmark

Delicately flavored with orange, these bar cookies are a holiday favorite in Denmark.

1/2 cup butter, softened	3 tablespoons grated orange peel
1-1/2 cups all-purpose flour	1 egg
1/4 cup sugar	4 oz. semisweet chocolate, melted

Lightly grease a large baking sheet; set aside. Preheat oven to 400F (205C). In a large bowl, press with the back of a spoon to blend butter into flour. Add sugar, orange peel and egg; stir in until a stiff dough forms. Refrigerate 20 minutes if dough is soft. On a lightly floured surface, roll out dough until 1/4 inch thick. Cut into 2'' x 1'' bars. Place on prepared baking sheet, 1 inch apart. Bake 10 minutes or until lightly browned. Dip 1 end of each baked bar in melted chocolate. Place on waxed paper until chocolate has set. Makes about 40 cookies.

MAIL-ORDER SOURCES

Aarikka Finland
See Scandinavia Center, Inc.

Bergquists Imports
1412 Highway 33 South
Cloquet, Minnesota 55720
(Mostly cookware, some foods)

Crate & Barrel (Also in Boston and Dallas)
850 N. Michigan Avenue
Chicago, Illinois 60611
($2 catalog; cookware, fabrics, glassware)

Erickson's Delicatessen
5250 N. Clark
Chicago, Illinois 60640
(Catalog; full range of foods)

Ingebretsen Scandinavian Center
1601 E. Lake
Minneapolis, Minnesota 55407
(Catalog; cookware, some foods)

Maid of Scandinavia Co.
3244 Raleigh Avenue
Minneapolis, Minnesota 55416
($1 catalog; cookware, some food products)

Norwegian & Swedish Imports
2014 London Road
Duluth, Minnesota 55812
(Cookware, foods)

Scandicrafts, Inc. (Wholesale)
P.O. Box 665
Camarillo, California 93011
(Cookware)

Scandinavian Center, Inc. (Wholesale)
401 Wynola Street
Pacific Palisades, California 90272
(Wooden & glass serving pieces)

Scandinavian Designs Unlimited
20 West Superior Street
Duluth, Minnesota 55802
(Serving and decorative pieces)

Williams-Sonoma Co.
Mail-Order Department
P.O. Box 7456
San Francisco, California 94120
(Catalog available; mostly cookware)

SCANDINAVIAN RECIPE TITLES

Denmark
AEblesalat 35, 46-47
AEbleskiver 122-123
AEblesuppe 26
AEg med Kaviar 17
Agurkesalat 99
Bondepige med Slør 119
Glaserede Kartoffler 74-75
Danablu med Frugt 19, 28
Farserede AEg 104, 110-111
Fiskefrikadeller 100-101
Flæskesteg 20
Flødeost med Jordbær 19, 28
Flødeost med Laks 18
Glaserede Champignon 39, 40
Glaserede Gulerødder 74-75
Grapefrugt med Krabbe 105
Havarti med Nødder 29
Havremelsbrød 33, 136, 137
Hindbærkager 149, 152
Hindbærsauce 108, 110-111
Julekage 132
Kaffeglasur 144
Kalkun 26
Karolines AEblekage 24
Karrysalat 98
Kaviar med Kartoffler 39, 40
Kringle 142-143
Krydrede Frikadeller 72
Kylling med Agurke 20-21
Laks 19, 27
Mandel Smørcreme 142
Mandelglasur 140
Mokkafromage 75
Nytårstorsk 78-79

Oksesteg med Løg 10, 21
Oksesteg 72-73
Orangesmåkager 154
Pandekager med Orangesmør 78
Rejer i Trængsel 18-19
Rødgrød 22-23
Rødkål 73, 74
Rombudding 108, 110-111
Romfromage 22
Rugbrød 135
Rygeost 100
Samsøsouffle 14-15
Sardin med Løg 26
Sennepssauce 77, 79
Sild med Løg 18-19
Skinke med AEg 28-29
Smørkage 144
Smørrebrød 16-29
Smørsauce 77
Snegle 139, 141, 143
Sommer Koteletter 35
Stegt Svinekam 116
Svinekam 39, 40-41
Tarteletter 71, 73
Tomater med Danablu 74
Vanille Smørcreme 139
Vanillekranser 23, 147
Wienerbrød 140-141
Wienerbrøds Kamme 139, 141, 143
Wienerfletning 144

Finland
Ananas Punajuurisalaatti 99
Ilmapuuro 119
Käärysyltty 52
Kalakukko 94-95
Karjalan Paisti 92
Karjalan Piirakka 90-91
Keitetyt Ravut 77
Klapsakkaa 11
Kurkkusalaatti 94, 110-111
Lehtisalaatti 91
Leipäjuusto 118
Linnunpesä 104-105
Lohipiirakka 86-87
Marja Kiisseli 92
Munajuusto 107, 110-111
Munavoi 92
Mustikkapiirakka 110-111, 153
Nissu Nassu 46-47, 147, 149
Pähkinäleivät 152
Paistettu Sienet 49
Pasha 42
Perunalanttulaatikko 46-47, 115
Pikkuleipienperustaikina 150
Porkkanalaatikko 110-111, 118
Pulla 133, 137
Rahkakuori 86
Riisipuuro 45
Rosolli 106, 110-111
Ruisleipä 134
Ruismarjapuuro 101
Sienisalaatti 117
Sima 57
Täytetty Tomatit 10-11
Tilliherneet 44
Tippaleipä 58

INDEX

Index

Index

8.426825990273